Extending Jenkins

Get a complete walkthrough of the many interfaces available in Jenkins with the help of real-world examples to take you to the next level

Donald Simpson

[PACKT] open source*

PUBLISHING   community experience distilled

BIRMINGHAM - MUMBAI

Extending Jenkins

First published: December 2015

Production reference: 1171215

Published by Packt Publishing Ltd.
Livery Place
35 Livery Street
Birmingham B3 2PB, UK.

ISBN 978-1-78528-424-3

www.packtpub.com

Credits

Author
Donald Simpson

Reviewer
Tony Sweets

Commissioning Editor
Amarabha Banerjee

Acquisition Editor
Indrajit Das

Content Development Editor
Riddhi Tuljapurkar

Technical Editor
Menza Mathew

Copy Editor
Kausambhi Majumdar

Project Coordinator
Sanchita Mandal

Proofreader
Safis Editing

Indexer
Tejal Daruwale Soni

Graphics
Abhinash Sahu

Production Coordinator
Melwyn Dsa

Cover Work
Melwyn Dsa

About the Author

Donald Simpson is an information technology consultant based in Scotland, UK.

He specializes in helping organizations improve the quality and reduce the cost of software development through the adoption of process automation and Agile methodologies.

Starting out as a Java developer, Donald's interest in application servers, networking, and automation led him to a career as a build engineer. He remains highly technical and hands-on and enjoys learning about new technologies and finding ways to automate and improve manual processes.

He can be reached at www.donaldsimpson.co.uk.

I would like to thank my wife, Clair, and my children, Freya and Lyla, for their support and encouragement throughout my career and the writing of this book.

About the Reviewer

Tony Sweets has over 20 years of experience in software development, with most of it in Java and Java-based technologies. Known as the "Tools" guy before there was any concept of DevOps, he also has a passion for setting up and managing hardware and networks. Introduced to Agile development very early on, he has set up and maintained his company's continuous integration system that ranges from Cruise Control to Hudson, and now Jenkins. He is currently a software architect in the payments field and has been working in financial services for over 17 years.

www.PacktPub.com

Support files, eBooks, discount offers, and more

For support files and downloads related to your book, please visit www.PacktPub.com.

Did you know that Packt offers eBook versions of every book published, with PDF and ePub files available? You can upgrade to the eBook version at www.PacktPub.com and as a print book customer, you are entitled to a discount on the eBook copy. Get in touch with us at service@packtpub.com for more details.

At www.PacktPub.com, you can also read a collection of free technical articles, sign up for a range of free newsletters and receive exclusive discounts and offers on Packt books and eBooks.

https://www2.packtpub.com/books/subscription/packtlib

Do you need instant solutions to your IT questions? PacktLib is Packt's online digital book library. Here, you can search, access, and read Packt's entire library of books.

Why subscribe?

- Fully searchable across every book published by Packt
- Copy and paste, print, and bookmark content
- On demand and accessible via a web browser

Free access for Packt account holders

If you have an account with Packt at www.PacktPub.com, you can use this to access PacktLib today and view nine entirely free books. Simply use your login credentials for immediate access.

Table of Contents

Preface

Jenkins provides many interfaces and extension points to enable users to customize and extend its functionality. In this book, we will explore these interfaces in depth and provide practical real-world examples that will take your usage of Jenkins to the next level.

In this book, you will learn how to develop and test your own Jenkins plugin, find out how to set up fully automated build pipelines and development processes, discover how to interact with the API and CLI, and how to enhance the user interface.

What this book covers

Chapter 1, Preparatory Steps, will cover the initial setup steps—getting your development environment set up, an overview of Jenkins and some options to install and run it as well as extend the basic setup. We will also review the principles of Continuous Integration, which are explored in greater detail later.

Chapter 2, Automating the Jenkins UI, will discuss how several common issues and bottlenecks may be alleviated through the automation and adaptation of the Jenkins frontend. Here, we will look at four fairly typical use cases, identify the root cause of the issues, and propose some possible improvements that can be made through the alteration and automation of the GUI.

Chapter 3, Jenkins and the IDE, builds on the Continuous Integration principals that we looked at earlier and provides an introduction to the Mylyn project.

It then details how to set up a process that enables developers to interact with Jenkins directly from within their IDE. A selection of examples covers Eclipse, NetBeans, and IntelliJ.

Chapter 4, The API and the CLI, illustrates how we can automate and extend Jenkins through its API and CLI. In this chapter, we will illustrate how to use these interfaces by working through the high-level "building blocks" of an example "Information Radiator" project.

This chapter will explain how to create a dynamic application that consumes information from Jenkins via its exposed interfaces.

We will also review other ways in which you could extend Jenkins via the CLI — by kicking off jobs and making other changes to Jenkins automatically and remotely.

Chapter 5, Extension Points, introduces many important concepts that provide a foundation for the Jenkins Extension points topics in the subsequent chapters. We will run through Java interfaces, Design by Contract, abstract classes, and Singletons. We will then take a look at how these patterns are used in the real world when we define our own Extension Point in Jenkins.

Chapter 6, Developing Your Own Jenkins Plugin, will combine the skills, concepts, and tools from the preceding chapters to build our first Jenkins plugin.

We will take a look at Maven and learn how to set it up and use it for Jenkins plugin development. We will then create our first Jenkins plugin, learn how to install it locally, and then learn how to quickly make, build, and deploy subsequent changes using Maven.

Chapter 7, Extending Jenkins Plugins, makes use of a simple plugin with the "Hello world" functionality we created in the previous chapter to keep the focus on getting to grips with the processes and tools. This chapter takes a look at the best way to get started with adding your own implementations. You will learn how to reuse existing code and functionality and understand how and where to find them.

After taking a look at some existing plugins and using those as examples, we will then take a detailed look at some of the additional resources and technologies you could take advantage of in your own projects.

Chapter 8, Testing and Debugging Jenkins Plugins, explains how to test and debug your own code and how to apply the same approach to existing plugins for troubleshooting.

It covers running tests with Maven, examines some existing tests from a popular plugin, and uses these to demonstrate how you can adapt these approaches to suit your own projects.

We will also take a look at debugging live code through the IDE and show how to integrate these useful functions into popular development IDEs. The final section of this chapter will introduce the inbuilt Jenkins Logger Console.

Chapter 9, Putting Things Together, takes a look at how Jenkins can be extended to work with other technologies and languages. We will start off with a look at the Jenkins Scripting console and see how useful it can be when combined with some Groovy scripting by providing some examples. We will then discuss developing applications using Groovy, Grails, and Gradle as possible alternatives to Maven and Java. The final part of this chapter covers Jenkins and Docker and then discusses how to set up build and deployment pipelines for iOS and Android development.

What you need for this book

The reader is assumed to have some working knowledge of Jenkins and programming in general, an interest in learning the different options to take things to the next level, and an inclination to understand how to customize and extend Jenkins to suit their requirements and needs.

Who this book is for

This book is aimed primarily at developers and administrators who are interested in taking their interaction and usage of Jenkins to the next level — extending it to fit their needs, interacting with Jenkins via its interfaces, and developing their own custom unit-tested plugins.

Conventions

In this book, you will find a number of text styles that distinguish between different kinds of information. Here are some examples of these styles and an explanation of their meaning.

Code words in text, database table names, folder names, filenames, file extensions, pathnames, dummy URLs, user input, and Twitter handles are shown as follows: "We can include other contexts through the use of the `include` directive."

A block of code is set as follows:

```
<html>
  <head>
    <meta http-equiv="refresh" content="5">
    <style type="text/css">
```

When we wish to draw your attention to a particular part of a code block, the relevant lines or items are set in bold:

```html
<html>
  <head>
    <meta http-equiv="refresh" content="5">
    <style type="text/css">
```

Any command-line input or output is written as follows:

```
java -jar jenkins-cli.jar -s http://minty:8080/ get-job VeryBasicJob
```

New terms and **important words** are shown in bold. Words that you see on the screen, for example, in menus or dialog boxes, appear in the text like this: "Note that the `http://jenkins-ci.org/` home page also hosts **Native Installers** for many popular operating systems under the **Native packages** column."

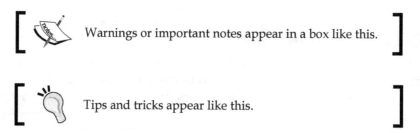

Warnings or important notes appear in a box like this.

Tips and tricks appear like this.

Reader feedback

Feedback from our readers is always welcome. Let us know what you think about this book — what you liked or disliked. Reader feedback is important for us as it helps us develop titles that you will really get the most out of.

To send us general feedback, simply e-mail feedback@packtpub.com, and mention the book's title in the subject of your message.

If there is a topic that you have expertise in and you are interested in either writing or contributing to a book, see our author guide at www.packtpub.com/authors.

Customer support

Now that you are the proud owner of a Packt book, we have a number of things to help you to get the most from your purchase.

Downloading the example code

You can download the example code files from your account at `http://www.packtpub.com` for all the Packt Publishing books you have purchased. If you purchased this book elsewhere, you can visit `http://www.packtpub.com/support` and register to have the files e-mailed directly to you.

Errata

Although we have taken every care to ensure the accuracy of our content, mistakes do happen. If you find a mistake in one of our books—maybe a mistake in the text or the code—we would be grateful if you could report this to us. By doing so, you can save other readers from frustration and help us improve subsequent versions of this book. If you find any errata, please report them by visiting `http://www.packtpub.com/submit-errata`, selecting your book, clicking on the **Errata Submission Form** link, and entering the details of your errata. Once your errata are verified, your submission will be accepted and the errata will be uploaded to our website or added to any list of existing errata under the Errata section of that title.

To view the previously submitted errata, go to `https://www.packtpub.com/books/content/support` and enter the name of the book in the search field. The required information will appear under the **Errata** section.

Piracy

Piracy of copyrighted material on the Internet is an ongoing problem across all media. At Packt, we take the protection of our copyright and licenses very seriously. If you come across any illegal copies of our works in any form on the Internet, please provide us with the location address or website name immediately so that we can pursue a remedy.

Please contact us at `copyright@packtpub.com` with a link to the suspected pirated material.

We appreciate your help in protecting our authors and our ability to bring you valuable content.

Questions

If you have a problem with any aspect of this book, you can contact us at `questions@packtpub.com`, and we will do our best to address the problem.

1
Preparatory Steps

In this first chapter, we will start off by looking at Jenkins from several different perspectives; how to obtain and run it, some of the ways and the reasons people use it, and what it provides to them. In doing so, we will take a look at some standard use cases and examine how a Jenkins installation will often evolve over a period of time—typically starting off with only the basic installation and core features, then progressively becoming more customized and advanced with different types of extensions. We will start off with "ready-made" plugins, and then progress towards extending these before looking at how to develop your own plugins.

We will then summarize the high-level aims of this book, and give the details of what you should hopefully gain from them.

We will provide an overview of the various tools and the environment setup that you will need in order to run the practical examples covered in the subsequent chapters, and we will review the best practices of **Continuous Integration** (CI) by identifying some of the ways that Jenkins can be used to achieve them.

Throughout this book, it is assumed that you already have some working knowledge of Jenkins, so we will not spend much time covering the basics, such as installing and starting Jenkins, or detailing the usage of standard features and core functions.

If you would like more details on these topics, there are numerous helpful tutorials and examples available online; the **Use Jenkins** section of the Jenkins homepage, `https://jenkins-ci.org`, is often a good starting point for help with general setup and usage questions.

Getting started with Jenkins

As a Java application, Jenkins can be installed and run in different ways depending on your requirements, personal preferences, and the environment that you are running it in.

The simplest and easiest approach to quickly get Jenkins up and running is by setting up Java, downloading the latest Jenkins WAR file from the Jenkins homepage (`www.jenkins-ci.org`), and then simply starting it from the command line like this:

```
java -jar jenkins.war
```

The following figure demonstrates the use of this approach by running just two simple commands:

1. `wget http://mirrors.jenkins-ci.org/war/latest/jenkins.war`:

    This command downloads the latest version of Jenkins from the main site.

    `wget` is a Linux utility that fetches files from the Web—if you are on a platform that does not have `wget`, you can simply save the link (the `jenkins.war` file) via your browser to a working directory instead.

    The URL is obtained by copying the **Latest & Greatest** link from the homepage at `https://jenkins-ci.org/`. Note that there is also an option to download and use the Long-Term Support release instead of the current, latest, and greatest, as explained here: `https://wiki.jenkins-ci.org/display/JENKINS/LTS+Release+Line`.

    This is preferable for more conservative installations, where stability is more important than having latest features.

2. `java -jar jenkins.war`:

    This second command tells Java to run the WAR file that we just downloaded as an application, which produces the resulting output that you can see in the following screenshot—Jenkins unpacking from the WAR file, checking and initializing the various subsystems, and starting up a process on port `8080`:

```
●●●                                    1. ssh
don@minty ~ $ wget http://mirrors.jenkins-ci.org/war/latest/jenkins.war
—2015-06-02 14:52:30—  http://mirrors.jenkins-ci.org/war/latest/jenkins.war
Resolving mirrors.jenkins-ci.org (mirrors.jenkins-ci.org)... 199.193.196.24
Connecting to mirrors.jenkins-ci.org (mirrors.jenkins-ci.org)|199.193.196.24|:80... connected.
HTTP request sent, awaiting response... 302 Found
Location: http://ftp-nyc.osuosl.org/pub/jenkins/war/1.616/jenkins.war [following]
—2015-06-02 14:52:30—  http://ftp-nyc.osuosl.org/pub/jenkins/war/1.616/jenkins.war
Resolving ftp-nyc.osuosl.org (ftp-nyc.osuosl.org)... 64.50.233.100
Connecting to ftp-nyc.osuosl.org (ftp-nyc.osuosl.org)|64.50.233.100|:80... connected.
HTTP request sent, awaiting response... 200 OK
Length: 63124136 (60M) [text/plain]
Saving to: 'jenkins.war'

100%[===============================================================

==============================================>] 63,124,136   836KB/s   in 1m 46s

2015-06-02 14:54:16 (582 KB/s) - 'jenkins.war' saved [63124136/63124136]

don@minty ~ $ java -jar jenkins.war
Running from: /home/don/jenkins.war
webroot: $user.home/.jenkins
Jun 02, 2015 3:11:02 PM winstone.Logger logInternal
INFO: Beginning extraction from war file
Jun 02, 2015 3:11:04 PM org.eclipse.jetty.util.log.JavaUtilLog info
INFO: jetty-winstone-2.8
Jun 02, 2015 3:11:06 PM org.eclipse.jetty.util.log.JavaUtilLog info
INFO: NO JSP Support for , did not find org.apache.jasper.servlet.JspServlet
Jenkins home directory: /home/don/.jenkins found at: $user.home/.jenkins
Jun 02, 2015 3:11:07 PM org.eclipse.jetty.util.log.JavaUtilLog info
INFO: Started SelectChannelConnector@0.0.0.0:8080
Jun 02, 2015 3:11:07 PM winstone.Logger logInternal
INFO: Winstone Servlet Engine v2.0 running: controlPort=disabled
Jun 02, 2015 3:11:07 PM jenkins.InitReactorRunner$1 onAttained
INFO: Started initialization
Jun 02, 2015 3:11:20 PM jenkins.InitReactorRunner$1 onAttained
INFO: Listed all plugins
Jun 02, 2015 3:11:20 PM jenkins.InitReactorRunner$1 onAttained
INFO: Prepared all plugins
Jun 02, 2015 3:11:20 PM jenkins.InitReactorRunner$1 onAttained
INFO: Started all plugins
Jun 02, 2015 3:11:20 PM jenkins.InitReactorRunner$1 onAttained
INFO: Augmented all extensions
Jun 02, 2015 3:11:23 PM jenkins.InitReactorRunner$1 onAttained
INFO: Loaded all jobs
Jun 02, 2015 3:11:24 PM hudson.model.AsyncPeriodicWork$1 run
INFO: Started Download metadata
Jun 02, 2015 3:11:24 PM org.jenkinsci.main.modules.sshd.SSHD start
INFO: Started SSHD at port 35218
Jun 02, 2015 3:11:24 PM jenkins.InitReactorRunner$1 onAttained
INFO: Completed initialization
Jun 02, 2015 3:11:24 PM hudson.WebAppMain$3 run
INFO: Jenkins is fully up and running
Jun 02, 2015 3:11:28 PM hudson.model.UpdateSite updateData
INFO: Obtained the latest update center data file for UpdateSource default
Jun 02, 2015 3:11:29 PM hudson.model.DownloadService$Downloadable load
INFO: Obtained the updated data file for hudson.tasks.Maven.MavenInstaller
Jun 02, 2015 3:11:29 PM hudson.model.DownloadService$Downloadable load
INFO: Obtained the updated data file for hudson.tasks.Ant.AntInstaller
Jun 02, 2015 3:11:31 PM hudson.model.DownloadService$Downloadable load
INFO: Obtained the updated data file for hudson.tools.JDKInstaller
Jun 02, 2015 3:11:31 PM hudson.model.AsyncPeriodicWork$1 run
INFO: Finished Download metadata. 7,238 ms
[]
```

Downloading and starting Jenkins

This simple process is usually all that is required to both download the latest version of Jenkins and get it up and running. You should now be able to access the web interface at `http://localhost:8080` through your browser and begin setting up jobs to make Jenkins work for you:

The Jenkins start page

Extending the basic setup

When you exit from the command prompt or shell that started the process that we looked at previously, the Jenkins instance will stop with the exit, so for anything beyond a very quick ad hoc test, some form of initialization or process management script is highly recommended. Such a script can also be easily tailored to perform a few "nice to have" functions for you, for example, things such as these:

- Starting up at system boot time
- Catering to `stop|start|restart|status` requests
- Redirecting console output to a log file so that you can monitor it for issues
- Running as a background/daemon process
- Running on a nonstandard port by setting the `--httpPort=` parameter, in cases where port `8080` is already used by another application
- Binding to a specific network interface, rather than the default `0.0.0.0` value using the `--httpListenAddress=` option

This Ubuntu-based example script from the home page demonstrates many of the previously mentioned features of Jenkins that is running under Tomcat. The script can be found at https://wiki.jenkins-ci.org/display/JENKINS/JenkinsLinuxStartupScript and is as follows:

```
#!/bin/sh
#
# Startup script for the Jenkins Continuous Integration server
# (via Jakarta Tomcat Java Servlets and JSP server)
#
# chkconfig: - 85 15
# description: Jakarta Tomcat Java Servlets and JSP server
# processname: jenkins
# pidfile: /home/jenkins/jenkins-tomcat.pid

# Set Tomcat environment.
JENKINS_USER=jenkins
LOCKFILE=/var/lock/jenkins
export PATH=/usr/local/bin:$PATH
export HOME=/home/jenkins
export JAVA_HOME=/usr/lib/jvm/java-6-sun
export JENKINS_BASEDIR=/home/jenkins
export TOMCAT_HOME=$JENKINS_BASEDIR/apache-tomcat-6.0.18
export CATALINA_PID=$JENKINS_BASEDIR/jenkins-tomcat.pid
export CATALINA_OPTS="-DJENKINS_HOME=$JENKINS_BASEDIR/jenkins-home
-Xmx512m -Djava.awt.headless=true"

# Source function library.
. /etc/rc.d/init.d/functions

[ -f $TOMCAT_HOME/bin/catalina.sh ] || exit 0

export PATH=$PATH:/usr/bin:/usr/local/bin

# See how we were called.
case "$1" in
  start)
        # Start daemon.
        echo -n "Starting Tomcat: "
        su -p -s /bin/sh $JENKINS_USER -c "$TOMCAT_HOME/bin/catalina.
sh start"
        RETVAL=$?
        echo
        [ $RETVAL = 0 ] && touch $LOCKFILE
```

```
             ;;
    stop)
             # Stop daemons.
             echo -n "Shutting down Tomcat: "
             su -p -s /bin/sh $JENKINS_USER -c "$TOMCAT_HOME/bin/catalina.
sh stop"
             RETVAL=$?
             echo
             [ $RETVAL = 0 ] && rm -f $LOCKFILE
             ;;
    restart)
             $0 stop
             $0 start
             ;;
    condrestart)
             [ -e $LOCKFILE ] && $0 restart
             ;;
    status)
             status -p $CATALINA_PID -l $(basename $LOCKFILE) jenkins
             ;;
    *)
             echo "Usage: $0 {start|stop|restart|status}"
             exit 1
esac
exit 0
```

Note that the http://jenkins-ci.org/ home page also hosts **Native Installers** for many popular operating systems under the **Native packages** column. These pages provide download links and installation instructions for each OS.

You may want to look at running Jenkins in a J2EE container too, which can often lead to a more seamless fit with your existing software stack and architecture. This may mean that you will inherit additional benefits, such as the container's logging, authentication, authorization, or resilience. Jenkins can be run with many popular J2EE compatible containers, including the following:

- WebSphere
- WebLogic
- Tomcat
- JBoss
- Jetty
- Jonas

There are more `init` script examples and detailed installation instructions readily available on the Web, which should cover any combination of operating system and container setup. The point of this is that you should be able to set up Jenkins to suit your environment and preferences.

For the purposes of this book, we will assume that Jenkins is being run directly from the command line on the local host. If you are using a J2EE container to host the application or running the application on a remote host, the only difference you will notice is that you may need to perform additional admin and deployment steps.

Jenkins evolution

Typically, most users or organizations will start off on their Jenkins journey by setting up a basic, standard Jenkins installation to manage a few simple development tasks. The most common use is to build your source code, either periodically or whenever it changes in your central repository (Git, Subversion, and so on).

Using Jenkins to automate this type of simple and repetitive task often provides a lot of useful benefits very quickly and easily. Straight out of the box, so to speak, you get a bundle of helpful features, such as task scheduling and job triggering, building and testing report pages, sending out email notifications and alerts when there are new issues, and providing rapid and live feedback of how healthy (or not!) your code base currently is. If you don't already have a tool in place to provide these things, then setting up a standard Jenkins instance will provide these initial basic features, which on their own may well transform your development process.

The next logical step after this is to gradually add a little more intelligence and complexity to the setup—does the code compile ok? How many unit tests have been passed now, how long does the application take to compile? Oh, and could we show on a web page who has changed which parts of the code base? Is our application running faster or better than it was previously, and is it stable? Even before we begin to add any type of extension or customization, the core Jenkins installation provides a plethora of options here—you can choose to build your application on any platform that runs Java (which means pretty much anywhere these days), and you can also do this in whatever way that suits you and your current setup the best, including using the standard and popular build tools such as Ant or Maven, and/or re-using your existing Ant or Maven build scripts, or your Linux Shell or Windows DOS scripts.

You can also easily set up a cross-platform environment by deploying Jenkins Slave Nodes, which will allow you to run different jobs on different hosts. This can be useful in the environments that use a combination of operating systems; for example, your application runs on Linux, and you want to run your browser-based tests using Internet Explorer on a Windows host.

This ability to act as an easily configurable "wrapper" for your existing process, combined with the flexible nature of Jenkins, makes it very easy to adapt your particular setup to suit your requirements with minimal change or interruption. This makes Jenkins far easier to implement than having to change your existing build and deployment processes and practices just to accommodate the requirements of a new tool.

After this stage, the benefits of setting up a Continuous Integration environment often become quite obvious: if we can automatically build our code and package our application so easily, wouldn't it be great if we could go on to deploy it too? And then, if we did that, we could automatically test how our new application performs on a replica of the target platform!

On reaching this point, Jenkins will be a pivotal tool in your Continuous Integration process, and the more you can extend it to suit your growing and specific requirements, the more benefit you will receive from it.

This leads us to extending Jenkins, which is what we will be looking at in the rest of the book.

The simplest way to extend Jenkins is through its fantastic and ever-expanding wealth of plugins. It is always recommended and informative to browse through them; existing plugins are frequently being improved upon and updated with new features, and new plugins are being added to the list all the time. We are going to do more than just review a few popular plugins here though — by the end of this book, you should have the ability to take your usage of Jenkins to the next level to create your own custom plugins and extensions and work with the many features and interfaces that Jenkins provides us with for extension and interaction.

We will be taking a detailed look at the following:

- The different ways in which we can use the existing features
- Interacting with Jenkins through its various interfaces and APIs
- How to interact with Jenkins from within your IDE
- Ways to build upon the existing functionality to suit your needs
- Developing, testing, and building your own custom Jenkins extension

Here are the main tools that we will be using to help us extend Jenkins, along with some information on setting them up, and the sources for further help and information if required:

- **Java Development Kit (JDK)**: You will need a version of this at the same bit level as your Java IDE, that is, both will need to be 32 bit or 64 bit, depending on your architecture and preference. You can choose from IBM, Oracle, or OpenJDK 6.0 or later. Each vendor supplies installation instructions for all major platforms.

- **Java IDE**: We will mainly be using Eclipse, but will cater to NetBeans and IntelliJ too, where possible.

    The most recent versions of each of these IDEs are available at their respective websites:

    - ° `https://www.eclipse.org/downloads/`
    - ° `https://netbeans.org/downloads/`
    - ° `https://www.jetbrains.com/idea/download/`

- **Mylyn**: This is used to communicate with Jenkins from our IDE. If Mylyn is not already included in your IDE, you can download it from the Eclipse site here: `http://www.eclipse.org/mylyn/downloads/`. We will cover this in detail in *Chapter 3, Jenkins and the IDE*.

- **Maven**: We will be using Maven 3 to build the Jenkins source code and our own custom plugin. Maven is a Java tool, so it will need to know about the JDK of your system.

- **Jenkins Source**: This will be downloaded by Maven.

- **Git**: On most Linux platforms, the equivalent of `sudo apt-get install git` should suffice. On Mac, there are several options, including the `git-osx` installer on Sourceforge. For Microsoft Windows, there is an executable installer available at `http://msysgit.github.io/`.

We will go in to more specifics on the installation and usage of each of these components as we use them in the later chapters.

Continuous Integration with Jenkins

Before we conclude this chapter, here is a list of the key practices of Continuous Integration (as defined by Martin Fowler in 2006) with the examples of the ways in which Jenkins can be used to help you achieve them:

- **Maintain a Single Source Repository**: Jenkins can interact with all modern source code and version control repositories—some abilities are built-in, others can be added as extensions.

- **Automate the Build**: As described earlier in the use cases, this is one of the core aims of Jenkins and often the main driver to start using Jenkins.

- **Make Your Build Self-Testing**: This is usually the second step in setting up a CI environment with Jenkins—once you automate the building of the code, automating the tests as well is a natural progression.

- **Everyone Commits To the Mainline Every Day**: We can't really force developers to do this, unfortunately. However, we can quite easily highlight and report who is doing—or not doing—what, which should eventually help them learn to follow this best practice.

- **Every Commit Should Build the Mainline on an Integration Machine**: Builds can be triggered by developer commits, and Jenkins Slave Nodes can be used to build and provide accurate replica environments to build upon.

- **Fix Broken Builds Immediately**: This is another developer best practice that needs to be adopted—when Jenkins shows red, the top focus should be on fixing the issue until it shows green. No one should commit new changes while the build is broken, and Jenkins can be configured to communicate the current status in the most effective way.

- **Keep the Build Fast**: By offloading and spreading work to distributed Slave Nodes and by breaking down builds to identify and focus on the areas that have changed, Jenkins can be tuned to provide a rapid response to changes—a good target would be to check in a change and obtain a clear indication of the result or impact under 10 minutes.

- **Test in a Clone of the Production Environment**: After compiling the new change, downstream Jenkins jobs can be created that will prepare the environment and take it to the required level—applying database changes, starting up dependent processes, and deploying other prerequisites. Using virtual machines or containers in conjunction with Jenkins to automatically start up environments in a known-good state can be very useful here.

- **Make it Easy for Anyone to Get the Latest Executable**: Jenkins can be set up to act as a web server hosting the latest version at a known location so that everyone (and other processes/consumers) can easily fetch it, or it can also be used to send out details and links to interested parties whenever a new version has been uploaded to Nexus, Artifactory, and so on.

- **Everyone can see what's happening**: There are many ways in which Jenkins communications can be extended — email alerts, desktop notifications, Information Radiators, RSS feeds, Instant Messaging, and many more — from lava lamps and traffic lights to the ubiquitous toy rocket launchers!

- **Automate Deployment**: This is usually a logical progression of the `Build -> Test -> Deploy` automation sequence, and Jenkins can help in many ways; with Slave Nodes running on the deployment host, or jobs set up to connect to the target and update it with the most recently built artifact.

The benefits that can be realized once you have achieved the preceding best practices are often many and significant — your team will release software of higher quality and will do this more quickly and for less cost than before. However, setting up an automated build, test, and deployment pipeline will never be enough in itself; the tests, environment, and culture must be of sufficient quality too, and having the developers, managers, and business owners "buy in" to the processes and practices often makes all the difference.

Summary

In this preparatory chapter, we have taken a look at the basics of Jenkins; how it is used from both functional and practical points of view. We have run through a high-level overview of the toolset that we will be using to extend Jenkins in the following chapters and reviewed the best practices for Continuous Integration along with the ways in which Jenkins can be used to help your team achieve them.

In the next chapter, we will take a look at the ways in which we can extend the Jenkins user interface to make it more productive and intelligent, and how we can extend the user experience to make life easier and more productive for end users, as well as for Jenkins admins, build scripts, and processes.

2

Automating the Jenkins UI

In this chapter, we will be looking at a selection of different approaches that can be used to alter and enhance the Jenkins **user interface** (**UI**).

As with Jenkins as a whole, the Jenkins UI is highly customizable and has been clearly designed from the outset to be adaptable and extendable so that you can tailor and adapt it to fit your particular requirements and environment.

There are different ways in which you can customize the UI, ranging from purely *look and feel* cosmetic alterations to user input refinements, and then towards the automatic creation of Jenkins jobs and setting up a dynamic Slave Node provisioning system.

The focus and the most suitable approach is usually driven by the way in which Jenkins will be used; focusing on the areas that matter the most in a particular situation is usually where the most benefit is to be gained.

We will examine four of the most common use case scenarios in this chapter and the different ways in which the automation and development of the Jenkins UI could be helpful for each case.

Use case scenario 1 – a large number of jobs

A single Jenkins instance can contain many jobs. The practical limit varies widely and depends on multiple factors, such as the following:

- Hardware resources such as RAM, CPU, disk, and network performance
- Slave nodes—how many there are, how they are set up, and their performance

- How well the jobs are distributed across the Master and Slave nodes
- Settings of individual jobs; their size, function, history, and retention

It's not unusual for a Jenkins instance to have over 1,000 jobs, or around 100 Slave nodes attached to a Master node.

Managing the performance load that this causes is a big task in itself, and Jenkins also needs to manage the presentation and housekeeping of these jobs — your users will not want to look through more than 1,000 jobs just to search for the one they need, and we also need to make sure that old jobs are cleaned up or archived and that new ones can be created both easily and accurately.

If you can reduce the number of jobs you require, then administration and resource overheads will be reduced as a result, and performance, usability, and reliability will also be increased, and the user experience will be improved.

Some planning and a little automation of the UI can often help us achieve this — let's take a look at a few scenarios and the possible solutions.

If the most pressing issue or bottleneck is that there are too many jobs, it would be helpful to first understand where the need for all these jobs originates, and then see what we can do about alleviating that.

Frequently, development teams work in Sprints and/or Releases. This usually means having a mainline development stream and one or more branch streams. Often this convention will be followed in Jenkins as well — we may want to set up Jenkins jobs to build and then deploy Sprint 3 or Release 49 code to integration environments, while deploying our mainline changes to CI and development environments. At the same time, there may be a logical or business requirement to support a production version of *everything,* just in case something goes wrong.

This could mean setting up jobs that are named accordingly, such as `Sprint 3`, and having this value hardcoded in the configuration with a pseudocode, something along the lines of *fetch the Sprint 3 war file and deploy it to the Sprint 3 server....*

These jobs will have a finite (and probably pretty short) life and will then need cleaning up or updating with new values for the next Sprint or Release. This type of regular and manual maintenance becomes a headache very quickly, which further increases the possibility of human error leading to the wrong thing being deployed to the wrong place.

One simple solution for this common scenario is to make use of Jenkins Environment Variables. If you navigate to **Manage Jenkins | Configure System | Global Properties**, you can create and define your own key-value pairs, which are immediately available to every job on any node:

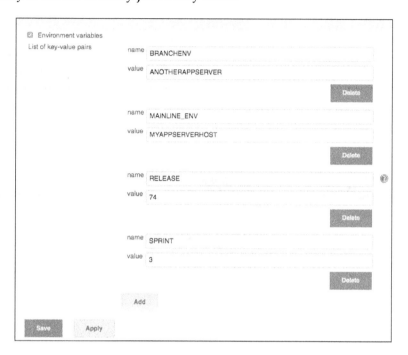

The preceding screenshot shows a few simplistic examples of the kinds of key-value pairs that you may want to set up—they can be whatever you like or need though.

Using this approach means that, rather than creating rafts of new jobs per Release or Sprint and catering to multiple concurrent Releases that will become obsolete shortly, you could just define two or three permanent sets of jobs that will pick up the key-value pairs from the location and use these to drive what they do—our job configuration pseudocode then changes. Initially, this in the form of the following:

fetch the Sprint 3 war file and deploy it to the Sprint 3 server…

This changes to something more generic along the lines of this:

fetch the ${SPRINT} war file and deploy it to the ${SPRINT} server…

This simple alteration to the approach can, in some circumstances, allow you to greatly reduce the number of Jenkins jobs by simply (and centrally) updating these Environment Variables to the new properties at the required point of your development life cycle—for example, at the end of a Release, Sprint, or Iteration cycle.

This one central configuration change will immediately update all of the jobs so that they can use these new values, and this approach could be extended to include information about many other aspects of build, test, and deployment processes, the branch location to checkout and build from, or the environment or host that the built artifacts should be deployed to, and so on. The following screenshot shows the Console Output page where the change is reflected:

If you need to create new jobs per Iteration, there are also ways in which you can automate the UI to simplify this process—we can use Jenkins to manage Jenkins.

If you take a look at your Jenkins home directory on the filesystem (as defined by the JENKINS_HOME variable), you will see the structure used to store the settings for each Jenkins job: each job is represented by a folder bearing the name of the job it represents, with each folder containing an XML file called `config.xml`. Each `config.xml` file contains the settings and information for that job.

There are normally several other files and folders too, such as a file to track the number of the next build (nextBuildNumber) and folders that are used to track and store history and artifacts created by previous builds.

The bare bones of a Jenkins job are, at its most basic form, as simple as this:

- A folder named after the job—for example, VeryBasicJob
- Inside this folder, a file called config.xml
- Inside this file, some XML along the lines of the following:

```xml
<?xml version='1.0' encoding='UTF-8'?>
<project>
  <actions/>
  <description>A bare-bones Jenkins job</description>
  <keepDependencies>false</keepDependencies>
  <properties/>
  <scm class="hudson.scm.NullSCM"/>
  <canRoam>true</canRoam>
  <disabled>false</disabled>
  <blockBuildWhenDownstreamBuilding>false</
blockBuildWhenDownstreamBuilding>
  <blockBuildWhenUpstreamBuilding>false</
blockBuildWhenUpstreamBuilding>
  <triggers/>
  <concurrentBuild>false</concurrentBuild>
  <builders>
    <hudson.tasks.Shell>
      <command>echo &quot;A very simple shell-based job&quot;</
command>
    </hudson.tasks.Shell>
  </builders>
  <publishers/>
  <buildWrappers/>
</project>
```

As you can see, this minimal job contains some very simple XML tags and data that detail the <description> and <command> tags, and various other settings used by Jenkins.

The Jenkins UI will interpret this folder and the XML file and display the **Config** page like this:

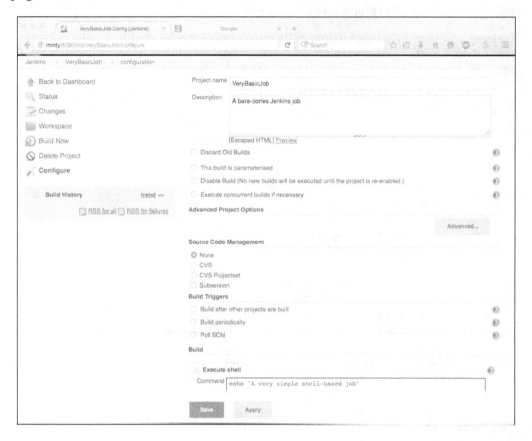

When the source configuration and the frontend UI are seen side-by-side just as you can see in the preceding screenshot, it becomes obvious that changing the XML file should change the job displayed by the UI and vice-versa.

So if we could automatically create these XML files and load them in to Jenkins somehow, we should then also be able to automate and do version control of all of our Jenkins jobs and allow end users to apply whatever customization they require at runtime, removing the need for manual intervention.

Fetching folder structures and XML files from Version Control, updating these XML files with user-selected values, and loading the resultant configuration into our Jenkins instance are just the sort of tasks for which Jenkins is the ideal tool—we can set up Jenkins to set up Jenkins!

In short, this process can be achieved by first *templating* your XML files—replace all references to the variable factors (such as references to **Release**, **Sprint**, **Hostnames**, and so on) with something easily identifiable. Then, create the Jenkins jobs that enable a user to specify what they would like to use in place of these placeholder values.

The next step is to perform some string replacement (using your preferred tool—**Perl**, **Sed**, **Awk**, and so on) to substitute the placeholder values with the user-selected ones, and then you just need to load the new configuration into Jenkins at runtime.

To demonstrate one possible approach to this, here is a basic functional shell script that does the job with comments explaining what's going on at each step. This uses the `Jenkins-cli.jar` file, which you can download and find out more about by going to your Jenkins instance and adding `/cli` to the URL, for example: `http://myjenkins.instance:8080/cli`.

Here you will also find detailed help and information on the many features and abilities that Jenkins offers.

```
# set up the variables required for this to work:
export JAVA="/usr/bin/java"
# Location & port of your Jenkins server
export HOST=http://myjenkinshost:8080

# location of the Jenkins CLI jar file
export CLI_JAR="/tool/ jenkins-cli.jar"

# a simple counter to track the number of jobs created
export COUNTER=0
# the location of the customized config.xml files to load
export WORKDIR="/home/jenkins_user/jobstoload"
# a simple for loop to iterate through each job:
for JobName in `ls $WORKDIR`
do echo "About to create job number ${COUNTER} with name ${JobName}"
${JAVA} -jar ${CLI_JAR} -s ${HOST} create-job ${JobName} <
$WORKDIR/${JobName}/config.xml
  echo "${JobName} created."
  let COUNTER++
  echo " "
done
```

This simple example, when set up in a Jenkins job, could be adapted to allow your users to create (or clean up) new Jenkins jobs quickly, easily, and reliably by pulling templates from version control and allowing the user to select from a predefined and valid set of options.

Use case scenario 2 – multiple hosts

The Jenkins UI can also be tailored to help in managing installations that require a large numbers of Slave hosts. This may be required to improve the performance of builds or test runs by distributing the load to other systems, or wherever Jenkins is used to perform functions spanning a multiple-host Operating System — something that Jenkins can do very easily through the built-in JNLP functionality.

Often, testing requirements dictate that a wide variety of different nodes running varying combinations of OSes and software are essential — this is common when you have an application that needs testing on different versions of Internet Explorer; each version requires a different Windows host, as each host can only support one version of the browser at a time.

Managing multiple and varying Slave Nodes can be problematic; however, the Jenkins UI provides several features that can help to simplify and automate this aspect.

One of the simplest approaches to manage instances with many Slave nodes is to use a Slave labeling scheme and a naming convention that describes the abilities or functions that the individual node perform.

To do this, you first need to label your Slave nodes — this can be done as and when they are created, or you can go back to existing Slave Nodes and label them as desired — note the multiple labels specified in the following Slave definition page:

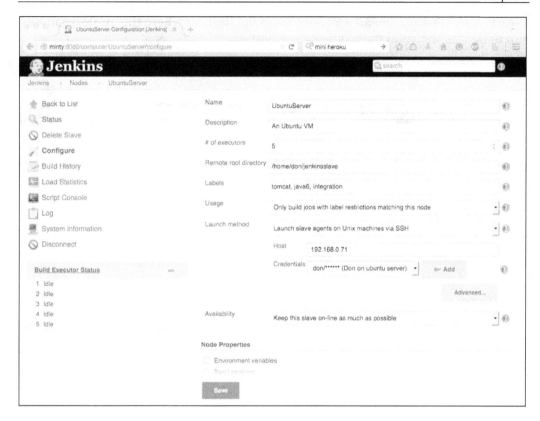

As you can see, this simple Slave has been given multiple labels of `tomcat`, `java6`, and `integration`.

We can now create or amend a job and select the **Restrict where this project can be run** option, as shown in the following screenshot:

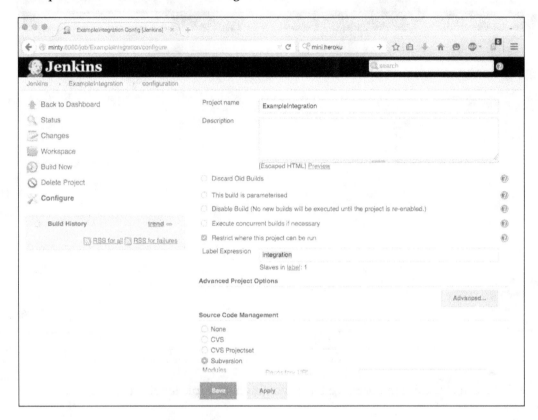

If we enter a label that matches one or more existing labels (integration in this instance), then this job will be run on a node matching this label. In cases where there are multiple matches, the job will be run on just one of the nodes.

This simple yet extremely powerful UI feature enables you to distribute the load across multiple nodes. The nodes may perform different functions, or they could be set up with different abilities — the labels can be whatever that helps you to decide what is best for your situation.

You could decide to distinguish between the physical characteristics of your nodes, such as those with a large free disk space, more memory or fast processors, or ones that have local databases or code deployments at the desired level, or with application servers or other supporting tools on them. This way you can not only distribute the load, but also maximize performance and reduce turnaround time by putting the right jobs on the hosts that are best suited for them, and by pooling your resources to fine-tune the response time of the various build tasks — getting the urgent tasks turned around as quickly as possible and leaving the less urgent jobs queued on a pool of dedicated servers.

This approach can be taken further using the Swarm plugin: `https://wiki.jenkins-ci.org/display/JENKINS/Swarm+Plugin`.

This plugin provides an added functionality that enables you to automatically provision and connect new Slave Nodes via a UDP broadcast that discovers and connects new nodes to the existing Master node, thereby creating an ad hoc cluster that you can tailor to meet demands.

You can use this to set things up so that when the build queue reaches a predefined threshold, new nodes will be dynamically provisioned and added to the pool of available nodes. You need to install the feature on the Master node and use the command-line client on the new Slave nodes.

Swarm nodes can also be assigned multiple labels at creation time through the `-labels` argument in the CLI. These values can additionally be set by the script that creates them; for example, the script could check for the existence of a local Oracle installation or a high percentage of free disk space and then use these results to decide which labels to apply to itself — `database`, `performance`, `java6`, `tomcat`, and so on accordingly.

Another very powerful tool for dynamic host provisioning and management is Docker, and, not surprisingly, there is a Jenkins plugin available for this too:

`https://wiki.jenkins-ci.org/display/JENKINS/Docker+Plugin`

Docker allows you to quickly and easily create and manage **Docker Images** that run in **Docker Containers**. These are quite similar in practice to virtual machines, but are smaller and of lighter weight, and therefore far quicker and easier to provision than traditional VMs.

Docker Images can also be version controlled via a **Docker Registry**, which works like a Git or Subversion repository for virtual machines; you can pull an existing Image from the Docker Index and update it to suit your requirements (as you would for a virtual machine—performing tasks such as deploying Tomcat, installing and configuring Apache, uploading some scripts, adding a version of Java, or installing Jenkins). Once you have customized your image, you can optionally push/publish it back to the index in exactly the same state that you created but under a new name, thus creating a template Slave that you can provision both rapidly and reliably to any platform that runs Docker. You can even run Docker on virtual machines—the possibilities that this approach provides are very interesting, and we will look at this in a little more detail in *Chapter 9, Putting Things Together*.

Use case scenario 3 – helping your users through UI automation

Customizing and automating the Jenkins user interface can help and empower users of your Jenkins instance to help themselves.

By ensuring that it is possible only for your users to input valid data, we can greatly reduce the risk of invalid input and the resulting issues, which should improve the user experience too.

The most common way to do this is to validate the user input at runtime. For example, if your job prompts the user to enter a day of the week or a build number, you may assign this to a variable called something like $WEEKDAY or $MY_BUILD_NUM respectively.

We can then set up our job to ensure that the supplied user data is valid—if the value of $WEEKDAY is not a valid day of the week, or the user has supplied the build number as `Build Two` instead of an integer value that we may have been hoping for, we can cause the build to fail with an error message explaining what the user has done wrong and how to correct it, rather than allowing our job to carry on regardless and letting it attempt to perform a function or create something that we know to be invalid.

It is also good practice and generally helpful for all concerned if you can let your users know what you expect—this is easily done by setting the description next to the input box like this:

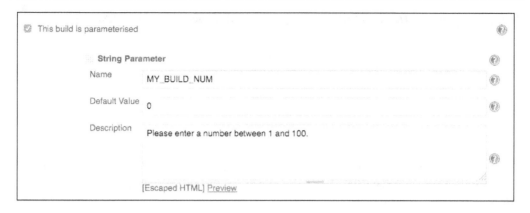

At runtime, this configuration will provide the user with a description of what we would like them to enter, and by setting a default value of 0, we can give them another hint.

This Jenkins job could then check that the value of $MY_BUILD_NUM is (as we'd hoped and requested) a numerical value greater than zero and less than 101, and then we can be reasonably happy that things are ok to continue.

It is often much safer to take the next logical step and restrict the options that are left open to the users. This further reduces the risks and also makes the experience nicer for the users — they may only run certain jobs occasionally, and expecting them to remember what you want may be a bit much to ask at times. This can be achieved by presenting them with a list of valid options and ensuring that they pick one of them:

The preceding information will be presented to the user at runtime like this:

This approach should hopefully be much more robust—so long as we remember to check that the value of ${WEEKDAY} is not equal to **Please Select...** before we attempt to use it!

This approach can be extended further by pulling in data from other sources and dynamically building up the options that are available to the user at runtime.

Another useful and more powerful example is the ability to populate a selection list with the values derived from current Subversion Tags.

This can be done through the **List Subversion Tags (and more)** option for parameterized builds. This allows you to present the user with a current list of available tags to select from—as an example, these tags could be created by other Jenkins jobs and may contain a list of candidate builds that the user can select from, to have a build deployed to an environment.

Suppose you have a Subversion repository with the following structure:

```
https://subversionrepo/mainproject/tags/Build_12.56
```

```
https://subversionrepo/mainproject/tags/Build_14.78
```

```
https://subversionrepo/mainproject/tags/Build_18.20
```

In this case, the user will be presented with a drop-down menu offering a choice of one of these three builds.

The option that the user selects is assigned at runtime to the variable that you created, say $BUILD_TO_DEPLOY, and your job can then use this selection to check out the requested build and deploy it using the SVN URL combined with the user's preferred option:

```
https://subversionrepo/mainproject/tags/${BUILD_TO_DEPLOY}
```

This functionality is provided as a part of the Subversion plugin, which is now a part of the core Jenkins build.

There are many other plugins and features that you can use to structure and improve your UI experience—the built-in Jenkins **Views** functionality allows you to create a dynamic list of jobs matching your criteria. This can be expressed as a simple regular expression so that all the matching jobs will be presented in one view. This works especially well when combined with a sensible naming convention for jobs.

Other approaches that may improve the user experience include setting up pipelines that manage job execution and flow. By setting up processes that the user can initiate easily, which will then carry on to work through a sequence of other jobs, the user only needs to trigger the first of several actions, like knocking over a line of dominoes, rather than trigger each build after checking that the previous build has completed and checking its stated output.

This can be achieved by simply using the built-in **Build other projects** option under **Post-Build Actions** for each job to create a simple sequence. Using the various trigger options, we can fine-tune things slightly so that certain jobs will stop the process if they have an issue, or can be set to carry on regardless, if appropriate.

If you would like to add more options, there are plenty of plugins readily available to help you. The Build Pipeline plugin offers some useful features, and the Join plugin can be incredibly useful. If you would like to run multiple jobs concurrently, then wait for them to complete before continuing and triggering the next job—as ever, there's a Jenkins plugin for most occasions!

Use case scenario 4 – UI tweaks

Sometimes Jenkins is set up and then left running in the background doing its thing; it's rarely checked upon or looked at unless things go wrong, and users are happy that things get done.

On other occasions, the Jenkins UI is used heavily by many people at the same time, all of whom will inevitably have their own requirements and priorities, and then the look and feel of Jenkins becomes a high priority.

There are many ways in which you can give the users what they want, including setting up numerous views, each providing a different user or group with a view of the (Jenkins) world that suits them.

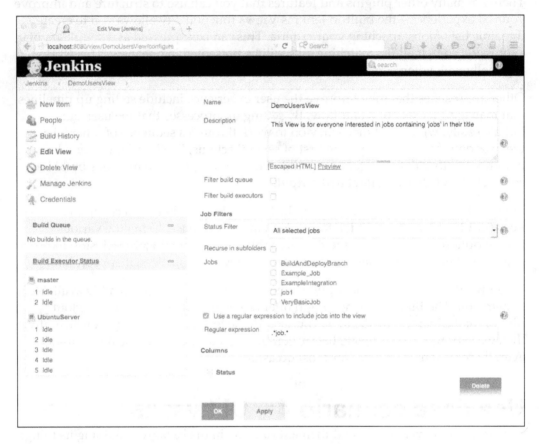

Using the simple `.*job.*` regular expression ensures that all jobs (both present and future) that contain the string `"job"` in their title will be displayed on this view. Again, this really relies on a decent naming convention being followed, but if this is done, it can reduce the maintenance requirements of this aspect to nothing—when a new matching job is created, it's automatically added to the view.

Plugins that provide further enhancements in this area include the Personal View plugin; as its name suggests, it enables users to create and manage their own view of the world, view **Job Filters**, and allows further tweaking. The **Chosen Views Tab** bar is helpful if you end up having too many Views and want to easily manage all of them on one screen!

Summary

In this chapter, we looked at the ways in which the user interface can be altered to suit your requirements. We looked at a few common issues and reviewed some possible approaches that could be used to alleviate them.

As you have seen, the Jenkins user interface is extremely powerful, and much of this power comes from its flexibility and extensibility.

Adapting the Jenkins user interface to address whatever use case applies to your environment can make a massive difference to the success of your Jenkins installation. At the same time, it also makes the user experience much more positive and can guide your users to interact with Jenkins in a mutually beneficial way. When it's easy for people to find what they want and hard for them to make mistakes (for example, due to runtime validation, dynamically populated forms, and automatically-created suites of jobs), you should have happier users and a more robust and efficient Jenkins too.

The in-built functionality of Jenkins can often provide enough flexibility to address whatever your most pressing Jenkins UI issues are; however, the wealth of available plugins allows you to quite easily take things much further should you wish to.

In chapters 6 and 7, we will revisit this topic in more detail when we look at extending the Jenkins user interface ourselves. We will see how you can develop and add your own customized GUI items directly to the Jenkins user interface, allowing you to extend things even further using Jelly, your own plugins, and the provided Jenkins extension points.

3
Jenkins and the IDE

In *Chapter 1*, *Preparatory Steps*, we took a high-level look at the basic principles and goals of Continuous Integration. We then walked through some fairly typical Jenkins use case scenarios to illustrate some of the ways in which extending Jenkins can help us to achieve these goals.

In this chapter, we will take a more detailed look at how to extend Jenkins and achieve the principles and goals of Continuous Integration. The focus of this chapter is to discover the ways in which we can help make things easier for software developers. The support and *buy in* of both the management and development teams is vital for the success of any good build process, and developers are obviously a fundamental part of any software development team.

We will take a look at some of the approaches that you can use to extend and adapt Jenkins to suit the specific needs and requirements of your developers, and we will demonstrate how adapting the way in which Jenkins information is presented to these developers can be customized to fit in naturally with the way they work. The intention here is to empower people with the tools that they find both beneficial and easy to use and to thereby encourage people to *do the right thing*, rather than try to make them do what we dictate using metrics, threats, nagging e-mails, and pointing the finger of blame every time a build fails—this is a sure way to end up with a lot of disgruntled developers who just want to keep their heads down!

Understanding motivations is the key to understanding behaviors, and, quite reasonably, developers are usually highly focused on developing code changes. They are usually not too interested in performing additional tasks, such as monitoring a build dashboard for updates or scrolling through a day's worth of e-mails to check whether someone else has recently broken the build before they commit their change. They are naturally focused on their role, their priorities, writing code and tests, and delivering them so that they can move on to pick up the next task. Anything that detracts or distracts from this goal may be seen as counterproductive. So, if we can extend Jenkins to simultaneously make things easier for developers to focus on the quality of their code and encourage them to *do the right thing* from a Continuous Integration point of view, everyone should be happier... well, that's the aim anyway.

The approach that I usually use to achieve this is best described by this quote:

> *"Make the wrong thing hard and the right thing easy."*
>
> -- *Ray Hunt*

It's a simple but effective mantra that I have found to really work in this kind of situation. Ray Hunt was the father of the natural horsemanship movement, and he used this philosophy with great success while training horses. And, between you and me, I have had some success when applying it to developers too!

The focus of this chapter, therefore, is to explore the ways in which we can extend Jenkins to provide our hardworking developers with the information they need to have in hand in a way that is natural and convenient for them to absorb, and makes it easy for them to *do the right thing*. If we can present our information directly in the IDE where they are already spending a majority of their time, hopefully we can achieve this.

Getting back to our Continuous Integration aims, from a developer-centric point of view, we are trying to encourage three main behaviors here:

1. **Commit frequently**: We can help here by making this easy to do using a suitable version control system that allows quick check-ins from within the IDE that the developers are using and by not distracting them from it to check on build tasks and statuses.

2. **If the build is broken, fix it as a top priority**: Making the current state very obvious will help to achieve this.

3. **Check the result of your actions**: This will greatly improve its functionality.

Rapid feedback and making it easy to see (and hard to miss it!) will help here too. If we can present all this information nicely and clearly from within the IDE that developers are already using, we should see some big improvements with little effort.

While the technologically focused solutions that we are about to run through should be helpful from our point of view, we can't expect them to be a miracle cure on their own. As mentioned previously, it takes a team working together to make these things work, so establishing and monitoring a set of developer best practices, publishing standards and guidelines, and providing user education and information, all play an important part in setting up an efficient and professional development team and productive build process IDEs, and Jenkins Build Connectors.

There are different development IDEs, and the selection depends on a number of factors, such as programming language (Java, C++, .Net, and so on), environment (Linux, Windows, Mac, and so on), and corporate and personal preferences (open or closed source). We will take a look at a few of the most popular IDEs and the solutions for them; however, there are many others as well that are available to suit different requirements.

Eclipse and Mylyn

The first and probably by far the most popular of all the development IDEs that we will look at is the Eclipse platform—this is extremely popular for a number of different projects including Java, C/C++, and PHP, and it has a vast user base and a wealth of mature and easily available plugins.

To achieve our goal of presenting Jenkins information to developers, Mylyn is currently the most popular extension that we can use in conjunction with Eclipse.

There is more information on Mylyn and the many features it provides at this link:

```
http://www.eclipse.org/mylyn/
```

The documentation at this link also states that Mylyn *reduces information overload and makes multitasking easy*, which sounds exactly like what we are looking for!

Installing Mylyn

Mylyn comes preinstalled with the most recent versions of Eclipse, so you may just need to select it by navigating to **Window | Show View | Other**, then selecting the **Builds** component from the **Mylyn** category like this:

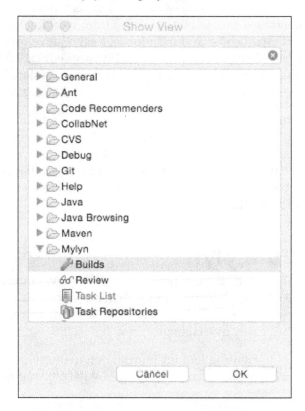

Now you just need to configure Mylyn using the following details:

If you use a version of Eclipse that does not come bundled with Mylyn, you can download and install it using the standard Eclipse installation process by selecting **Help | Software Updates...** then add a new update site with this URL: `http://download.eclipse.org/tools/mylyn/update/e3.4` (or a later version, if available and preferred).

Once this has been done, select the new update site that you just created and add the Mylyn components you would like to install.

Mylyn and Jenkins configurations

Once installed, you will then be able to select **Window** from the main toolbar menu, and then **Show View**, **Mylyn**, and **Builds**.

This should produce a window similar to the following, from which you can then select the highlighted option to create a new build server definition:

This produces a new wizard:

After selecting the **Hudson** option and clicking on **Next**, you are presented with a **Server Properties** dialogue where you can define and configure the properties for **New Build Server**:

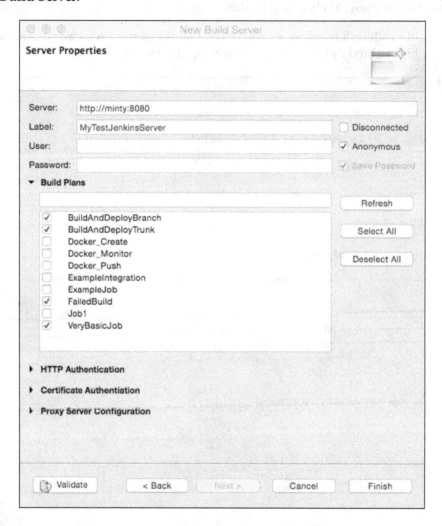

Here you can specify the URL and the credentials required for your Jenkins server. A quick refresh should show a successful connection to your Jenkins instance and also pull back a list of job definitions for you to select from. Note that Mylyn caters to a host of other connection and authorization features here, which you can configure if required.

After a quick check using the **Validate** button, click on **Finish** to save and close the server configuration.

This should result in a new **Builds** window displaying live information on the jobs that you have selected from your Jenkins server, something similar to this:

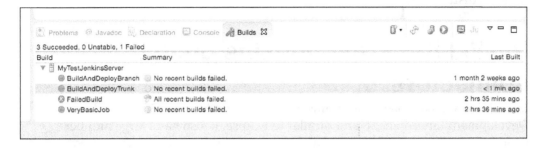

Exploring the options in this window shows that you can right-click and select a number of functions to perform on a selected job:

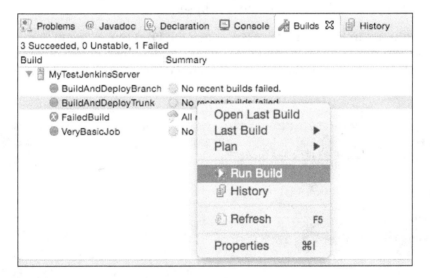

You can perform the following functions:

- View the history for a selected job
- Open the job in a browser inside Eclipse
- Run the selected job
- View the console output for the last run
- Show the JUnit results in the JUnit view

All of these can be done directly from within the Eclipse IDE, making it very easy for developers to keep an eye on the things they need to know with very little effort and minimal distractions.

IntelliJ IDEA and Jenkins build connectors

IntelliJ IDEA, developed by JetBrains, is another very popular Integrated Development Environment, and, similar to Eclipse, it also has a large number of add-ons and plugins that are available to extend its use and functionality.

In this section, we will take a quick look at installing and configuring the **Jenkins Control Plugin** for IntelliJ IDEA, and we will configure it to provide a functionality similar to that provided by Mylyn under Eclipse.

Installing plugins in IntelliJ is very easy—open the **Preferences** menu item, then select **Plugins** on the left-hand side menu. The Jenkins Control plugin is not currently bundled with the IDE, so click on the **Browse repositories...** button as shown in the following screenshot:

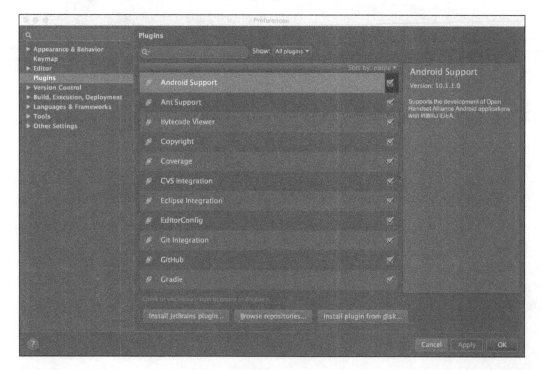

This opens up a new subwindow where you can enter Jenkins in the search dialogue to find the two (currently) available plugins, as follows:

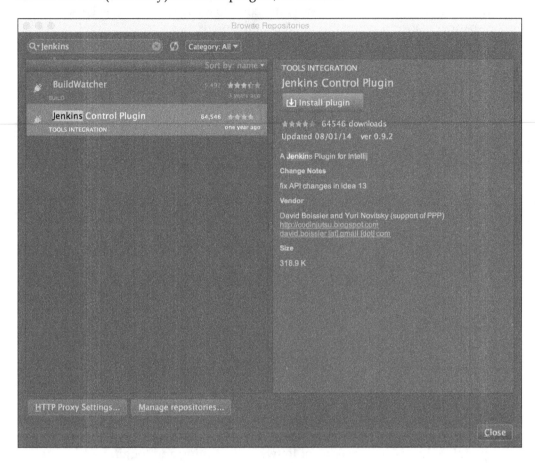

Click on the green **Install Plugin** button — the plugin will be downloaded and you will be prompted to restart IntelliJ IDEA — this completes the installation.

After restarting the IDE, click on the **View** menu, select **Tool Windows**, and you should see a new **Jenkins** option. Selecting this produces a new pane entitled **Jenkins**, where you can configure the connection to a Jenkins server by clicking on the spanner icon and filling out the requisite details:

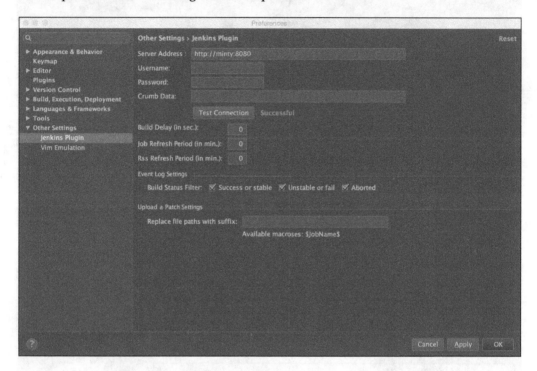

My example Jenkins instance is very simplistic — you will probably want to use authentication on a real Jenkins instance and therefore, will need to fill out the corresponding details. You may want to tweak the timing and logging settings to suit yourself; however, the basic setup is very simple and also very similar to the earlier Mylyn example.

Once done, hit the **OK** button, and you should see a view of your Jenkins instance inside IntelliJ:

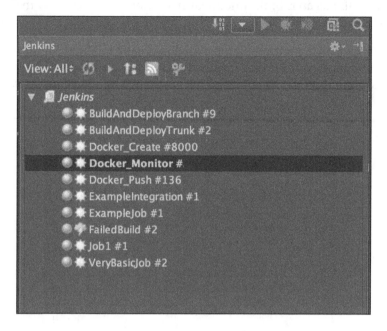

As with Mylyn, you can perform several useful functions using this plugin—monitoring the status of builds, triggering new builds, and viewing the results and history of the selected jobs.

NetBeans

The NetBeans IDE has an inbuilt functionality to monitor Jenkins via the `HudsonInNetBeans` service.

Selecting the **Services** tab within NetBeans will reveal a Hudson Builders item where you can define your Jenkins instance and configure which items you would like to monitor based on the View definitions available on your Jenkins server:

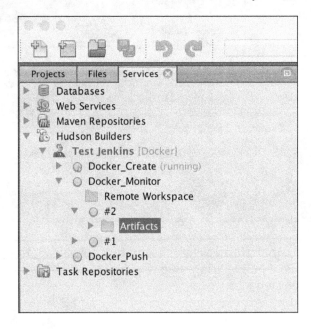

Once you have registered the server, you will be notified of any failures by a popup within the IDE. You can read more about the functionality and configuration of this extension here: `http://wiki.netbeans.org/HudsonInNetBeans#General_setup_and_view`.

In addition, the Build Monitor plugin can also be added to include status bar notifications—it can be downloaded from the plugin home page here: `http://plugins.netbeans.org/plugin/814/build-monitor`.

Then, the plugin is installed from **Tools | Plugins** menu item by selecting the **Downloaded** option and navigating to the recently downloaded file with an .nbm extension:

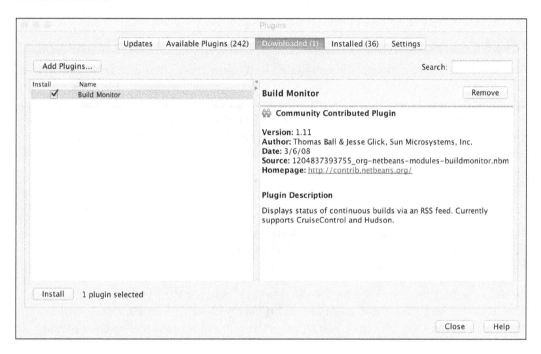

Now, simply select **Install**, agree to the terms, and click on **Install** again—once complete, click on **Finish**. You should now have a status bar item that can be configured to monitor the status of one or more of your Jenkins jobs, thus, providing another useful and unobtrusive mechanism to keep an eye on more important builds.

Summary

In this chapter, we looked at the key aims of Continuous Integration and how they specifically relate to developers. We have reviewed what we want to achieve in this area and how we can do so, that is, by enabling developers to easily do the right thing and by making their lives and roles easier.

There are many different options available that allow us to integrate Jenkins and the developers' environment, and we have detailed some popular examples of three of the most popular IDEs—there are many other options available for these IDEs and for others too. If the preceding options don't fit with your environment, hopefully the general idea and approach will translate to something that suits you. These plugins are being developed and enhanced on a regular basis, so pick the approach and the combination that works best for you and your environment. The key aim is to make life easy for others and encourage them to make your life easier too!

Also, there are many other ways in which we can communicate Jenkins information to others besides the IDE; there are system tray notifiers, Information Radiators, dashboards, custom web apps, e-mail alerts, instant message notifications, and even automated lava lamps, and foam-rocket launchers!

In the next chapter, we will take a look at several other ways in which we can interact with Jenkins—these are more technical and less end user-focused, but are related in a way that may give you some alternative ideas to develop your own bespoke solutions.

4
The API and the CLI

In the previous chapter, we looked at several ways in which we can interact with Jenkins and extend its use so that developers can benefit directly from within their development environments.

The plugins and add-ons that we looked at were obviously, somehow, able to fetch "live" data from Jenkins in order to convey this data directly to the client environment (the developers' IDE).

In this chapter, we will take a look at how these plugins were able to access this information, and we will explore the various mechanisms and interfaces that Jenkins provides for programmatic interactions, for example, the Jenkins **Application Programming Interface (API)**. We will also explore the Jenkins **Command-line Interface (CLI)**, which offers a mechanism by which you can remotely interact with Jenkins programmatically and/or interactively.

Both these features are extremely powerful and are the fundamental utilities to extend Jenkins.

There are three main functions for which you would normally use the Jenkins API; these are as follows:

- Retrieving and consuming information from Jenkins
- Triggering builds based on external events
- Creating, copying, and altering the Jenkins configuration

Creating an Information Radiator with the Jenkins XML API

In order to illustrate how you can use the Jenkins API to extract live information from Jenkins programmatically, we're going to take a high-level look at a practical example—creating an Information Radiator that fetches Jenkins information and displays it in an external web page. We will not be writing all of the code for this in detail; however, we will analyze the basic building blocks in sufficient detail so that you are able to adopt the general approach and develop your own customized solution in the language of your choice.

Information Radiators are simple but useful *live* web pages that allow people to easily monitor the status of your most crucial Jenkins jobs in real time. This is quite similar to the IDE plugins we looked at earlier, but instead these indicators are displayed on television screens in an office to radiate the information

The convention for Information Radiators is to *keep it simple*—to have as few jobs as possible and have them display a green indicator if everything is alright and a red indicator if there is an issue. Sometimes it's useful to show an amber indicator if the build is in progress. This simple system helps to highlight the urgent issues that need to be fixed as a top priority, and it also serves to deter people from checking in new changes when they can clearly see that the build is not currently stable; adding further alterations to an already broken system will only compound the issue.

In our high-level walkthrough, we will monitor the current state of just one Jenkins build. You will be able to reuse and extend the same approach to monitor as many builds as you want to, and you will see how you can additionally pull in and report other details from your Jenkins jobs.

Note that there are many prebuilt solutions that you could use for this, including a variety of plugins for different needs—we are deliberately taking a DIY approach here in order to demonstrate the possibilities and show you how to use the Jenkins API.

Getting the information from Jenkins

The first step is to get our (programmatic) hands on the information. The simplest way to do this is via the XML API. This simply involves appending the `/api/xml` string to the URL for the job you would like to monitor, as shown here: `http://yourjenkinsserver:8080/job/YourJob/api/xml`.

Note that there is also a JSON API available; if this suits your needs better — simply replace `api/xml` with `api/json` to receive the same information in the JSON format.

If you do this in a browser, you should see XML somewhat similar to my **VeryBasicJob** job:

The text returned by the API is simple and the XML is quite self-explanatory; a quick look through it shows that it contains all the information that you would want on the job you just queried — it just needs to be processed and interpreted. There doesn't seem to be much available in the way of documentation for these XML elements; however, if you start off with as simplistic a job as possible and then make changes and additions to that, you should be able to figure out what each element does and what the possible values can be.

An XML processor is the best way to handle this, and your scripting or programming language of choice should provide you with several options to choose from. For example, Perl has **XML::Simple**, Python has **ElementTree**, there is **XmlParser** for Groovy, and **JAXP** for Java, amongst many others. If you don't have any of these, you could use `grep` and `awk` to find the line and the values you want in a shell script.

So, we now have a job that we would like to monitor, some way to fetch all the current information on this job, a suitable method to handle the XML, and a mechanism to extract the information we want.

For this example, all that we really want to know about is the current state of the build — the values that correspond to our red, amber, and green health indicators — and these are present in the XML example as the current `color` attribute of the job.

For example, consider the following XML tag: `<color>blue</color>`. This shows that we currently have a non-running and stable job, whereas `<color>blue_anime</color>` refers to the blue and animated health indicator icon for a job that was healthy for the last build and is currently building.

We can simply show any mention of `anime` as amber in our Radiator. Both `<color>red</color>` and `<color>red_anime</color>` are the obvious equivalents for failed and running (but previously failed) jobs respectively. If you take a look at the XML for a variety of different job types and states, you will be able to spot and interpret the naming conventions used — just add `/api/xml` to a varied selection of jobs and compare them.

Automating the job

The next hurdle for our simple Information Radiator is automating and scheduling the job, and, as you'd expect, we can do this very quickly and easily in Jenkins.

Just create a new Jenkins job that fetches the corresponding URL (with `/api/xml` at the end) and feed this to your XML parsing script to extract the current values.

Many programming and scripting languages have a built-in XML or web fetching abilities, but if you prefer, you can use curl or wget to fetch the data and then pass this to your script.

The Jenkins job can be scheduled to run at a frequency that suits you—you can do this through the inbuilt cron function using the standard cron notation; for example, you can set your job to run every two minutes, as follows:

In this entry, I have specified H/2 * * * * to have this job run every two minutes. The symbol H, is a handy Jenkins inbuilt mechanism that allows Jenkins to balance and manage job scheduling. Rather than trigger all the jobs at exactly the same time, Jenkins is able to distribute the load for you. For more details, click on the ? icon next to the **Schedule** input box, which states the following:

To allow periodically scheduled tasks to produce even load on the system, the symbol H (for hash) should be used wherever possible. For example, using 0 0 * * * for a dozen daily jobs will cause a large spike at midnight. In contrast, using H H * * * would still execute each job once a day, but not all at the same time, better using limited resources.

If you are unfamiliar with the cron syntax, take a look at the cron man page (type man cron in a terminal) on any Linux box. There are also several helpful cron generators online, such as this one at http://crontab-generator.org/, which can be very useful.

Please note that it is highly recommended that you test and fine-tune your job *before* deciding on and setting a frequency for repeated builds. For example, if your job takes 3 minutes to run and you set it up to run every minute, things will not go well!

The last remaining task for this step is to store the data somewhere—I usually prefer a simple MySQL database, which I can update at the end of a job simply by passing the current runtime parameters to the MySQL binary.

Radiating the information

The final step is to display the information from the database as a color "radiator"—this simply involves producing a web page that queries the data and translates this information to the appropriate color—red, amber, or green. This can be done in many languages, including PHP, JSP, and ASP if you like, but the simplest approach may be to have your Jenkins job write out the raw HTML to a file for you, perhaps something like this:

```html
<html>
  <head>
    <meta http-equiv="refresh" content="5">
    <style type="text/css">
      .myclass{
        width:270px;
        height:150px;
        position:absolute;
        left:50%;
        top:50%;
        margin:-75px 0 0 -135px;
      }
    </style>
  </head>
  <body style="background:#088A08">
    <div class="myclass">Status of my VerySimpleJob</div>
  </body>
</html>
```

With the job updating the value for the background color as suitable. Note that there's a Meta refresh tag in the preceding code to reload the page every 5 seconds—you will need to implement something like this, otherwise you will be looking at the same information for a long time!

Jenkins as a web server – the userContent directory

You can even get Jenkins to act as a simple web server and host the web page we created for you—if you copy the file that is produced by the job to the userContent directory that is within your JENKINS_HOME location on the system that runs your Jenkins instance, you will see the file appear at this URL: http://myjenkins:8080/userContent

This should look as follows:

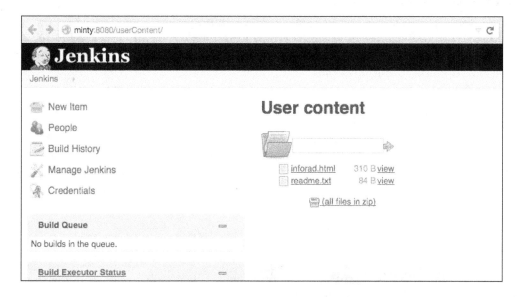

Clicking on the **inforad.html** link will give you the following page—our very simple DIY Information Radiator:

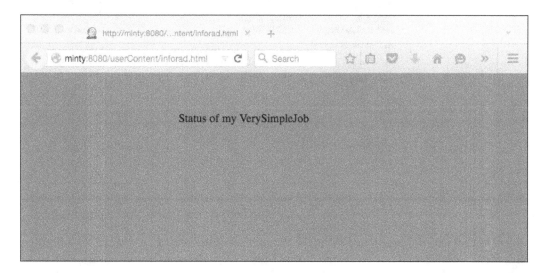

This simple exercise illustrates how you can query Jenkins via the API to retrieve and consume information in real time.

The Jenkins CLI

In this section, we will review the Jenkins CLI—this is another Jenkins extension point that can be extremely useful in certain situations—typically it is used to run commands against a remote Jenkins server, performing functions such as triggering builds or updating configurations.

How to set it up

In order to use the Jenkins CLI, you need the "jenkins-cli.jar" file.

This can be quickly and easily fetched from your own Jenkins server. If you append "/cli" to the web address of your Jenkins instance, you should see a page similar to this:

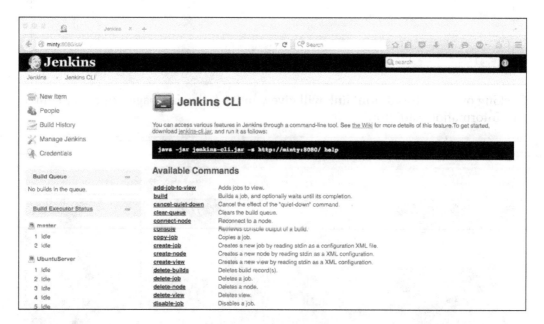

This URL provides everything you should need to get started with the Jenkins CLI.

There is a link to the Jenkins Wiki topic for further information, a direct download link for the Jenkins-cli.jar file from your server (http://{yourserverand:port}/jnlpJars/jenkins-cli.jar), and a list of available CLI commands along with brief descriptions.

How to use it

Once you have saved the CLI jar locally (you can download it via the browser or use a command-line tool, such as `wget` or `curl`), you just need to have your Java environment set up and then execute the line detailed at the start of the help page, as follows:

```
java -jar jenkins-cli.jar -s http://{yourserverand:port}/ help
```

Assuming that you have the `Jenkins-cli.jar` in the current directory and you updated the address to reflect your server, you should get back the basic help information, and you are good to go.

Triggering remote jobs via the CLI

The most common and perhaps the simplest task of the CLI is triggering a remote job to run at a certain point in a process. This can be extremely useful when you are integrating Jenkins with other legacy systems and gradually introducing automation to a manual process. You may not be able to automate everything straight away, or have Jenkins control everything all at once, but if you can set up a Jenkins job to automate individual parts of an existing manual workflow, you can then introduce Jenkins gradually and work towards removing the manual steps from the chain piece by piece.

For example, say we have a legacy batch job that runs some form of data processing. This processing may take some time to run, and there may be another step that comes along and checks whether the processing is complete, and if so, then transfers the new data to another location or passes it to another process. We can start off by creating a Jenkins job that, when called, picks up the data, checks whether it is valid, and then passes it to the next part of the process. This may remove a manual step and reduce the overall processing time. But how does the Jenkins job know when to run? It may not be efficient or possible to tell whether the processing has completed, but we can make a small update to the process to invoke the Jenkins job automatically after the initial processing.

To remotely trigger a job to run on a simplistic Jenkins server is as easy as this:

```
MacDonald:jenkinscli donaldsimpson$ curl -O http://minty:8080/jnlpJars/jenkins-cli.jar
  % Total    % Received % Xferd  Average Speed   Time    Time     Time  Current
                                 Dload  Upload   Total   Spent    Left  Speed
100  769k  100  769k    0     0  1168k      0 --:--:-- --:--:-- --:--:-- 1167k
MacDonald:jenkinscli donaldsimpson$ java -jar jenkins-cli.jar -s http://minty:8080/ build VeryBasicJob
MacDonald:jenkinscli donaldsimpson$ []
```

Here, we are first downloading the Jenkins CLI jar file to the current directory using `curl`:

```
curl -O http://minty:8080/jnlpJars/jenkins-cli.jar
```

This step needs to be done only once. We will then invoke the remote job with this command:

```
java -jar jenkins-cli.jar -s http://minty:8080/ build VeryBasicJob
```

Using this simple configuration, you will get no feedback of what happens; however, checking out `VeryBasicJob` on the Jenkins server should reveal that the job was triggered, and in the console output, it should also mention the following:

Started from command line by anonymous

So, we can see that this has worked ok, but the lack of feedback isn't very helpful. If we add the `-s` and `-v` arguments to the command, we will get the complete details of what is going on, as follows:

```
MacDonald:jenkinscli donaldsimpson$ java -jar jenkins-cli.jar -s http://minty:8080/ build VeryBasicJob -s -v
Started VeryBasicJob #9
Started from command line by anonymous
Building on master in workspace /home/don/.jenkins/jobs/VeryBasicJob/workspace
[workspace] $ /bin/sh -xe /tmp/hudson8829646407690621878.sh
+ echo A very simple shell-based job
A very simple shell-based job
+ sleep 20
Finished: SUCCESS
Completed VeryBasicJob #9 : SUCCESS
MacDonald:jenkinscli donaldsimpson$ []
```

This looks much better—we can now see that we have kicked off run #9 of `VeryBasicJob`, which simply sleeps for 20 seconds before exiting successfully.

This output information could be used in the client scripts to check for a success or failure, or you could make a note of the job number, or record any other output that would be useful to know.

Obviously, we wouldn't normally run Jenkins without some form of authentication in place, so in the real world things will be a little bit more complex. The user for whom you are running the CLI commands first needs to be granted the "Overall/Read" account permissions in the configure user page of Jenkins. You can then simply add the user name and password at the end of the command line, as shown here:

```
--username don --password MyPassword123
```

This is enough to get things working, but it's still not great from the security point of view; the credentials will be visible in plain text in the script that you add them to, or within the history of the shell you have used, or within the HTTP stream if you are not using HTTPS. The credentials may also be visible as args that are passed to the running process when users run `ps` or `top`, and so on, on the same host.

A more secure method is to set up SSH keys and pass in the private key for the public key. If you go to "configure" in Jenkins for your user name, you can set up the SSH keys for your account in the textbox provided. There are detailed instructions on setting up SSH here:

```
https://help.github.com/articles/generating-ssh-keys/
```

Once this is done, depending on the version of Jenkins you are using, Jenkins may automatically check for and use your SSH credentials from any of the following locations:

```
~/.ssh/identity, ~/.ssh/id_dsa, ~/.ssh/id_rsa
```

Then, you can explicitly supply the path to the key as follows (appending this to the command line instead of the earlier user name and password details):

```
-i ~/.ssh/id_rsa
```

For jobs that require parameters (that is, those that you have set up to request information from the user at runtime), you can supply additional "-p" arg(s), as shown here:

```
-p sprint=1.7
```

This will be passed to the job exactly as if the user had entered the data via the user interface and assuming there was an input element named "sprint" configured for that job.

Updating Jenkins configuration

Another very useful ability of the Jenkins CLI is to update the Jenkins configuration programmatically and remotely.

From the help page, we saw when we appended /cli to the server URL earlier that the two commands, get-job and create-job, can be very useful.

Running get-job will request Jenkins to supply the XML definition for that job.

For example, consider the following command:

```
java -jar jenkins-cli.jar -s http://minty:8080/ get-job VeryBasicJob
```

When this is run in my server, it will return the following output:

```
MacDonald:jenkinscli donaldsimpson$ java -jar jenkins-cli.jar -s http://minty:8080/ get-job VeryBasicJob
<?xml version='1.0' encoding='UTF-8'?>
<project>
  <actions/>
  <description>A bare-bones Jenkins job</description>
  <keepDependencies>false</keepDependencies>
  <properties/>
  <scm class="hudson.scm.NullSCM"/>
  <canRoam>true</canRoam>
  <disabled>false</disabled>
  <blockBuildWhenDownstreamBuilding>false</blockBuildWhenDownstreamBuilding>
  <blockBuildWhenUpstreamBuilding>false</blockBuildWhenUpstreamBuilding>
  <triggers/>
  <concurrentBuild>false</concurrentBuild>
  <builders>
    <hudson.tasks.Shell>
      <command>echo &quot;A very simple shell-based job&quot;
sleep 20</command>
    </hudson.tasks.Shell>
  </builders>
  <publishers/>
  <buildWrappers/>
</project>MacDonald:jenkinscli donaldsimpson$ []
```

This XML can be also redirected to a file by appending "> VeryBasicJob.xml" to the end of that command for example, and the file can then be added or updated in your Version Control software as a periodic backup.

Similarly, you can choose to create a new job using the create-job command like this:

```
java -jar jenkins-cli.jar -s http://{yourserverand:port} create-job
MyNewJobName < MyNewJob.xml
```

The MyNewJob.xml file can, for example, be created programmatically via a combination of a Jenkins job, an XML template, and some user-specified input.

We could also update an existing job using update-job in conjunction with an existing job name:

```
java -jar jenkins-cli.jar -s http://{yourserverand:port} update-job
VeryBasicJob < VeryBasicJob_v2.xml
```

This approach can be used to build a mechanism that will back up all or some of your Jenkins configuration to Version Control, and then, reload them programmatically (via Jenkins).

You can also expand this approach to perform some modifications to the XML files (and therefore, the job configurations they create) if changes are required; for example, updating the release or sprint details periodically.

Summary

In this chapter, we explored the possibilities that the Jenkins API and the Jenkins CLI open up.

We have worked through some high-level examples and illustrated how you can go about developing your own bespoke Information Radiator using the XML API.

We have also outlined some of the functionalities provided by the CLI and demonstrated how you can use them.

As you can see from the openness of both of these features, the flexibility of Jenkins is quite amazing—it's an open platform that provides you with numerous ways of adapting and extending it to suit your needs and requirements, whatever they may be.

The way in which the plugins that we examined earlier were able to show live information on a remote Jenkins server is now hopefully quite obvious, and we will take our usage of the API and CLI still further when we later look at how to develop our own plugins for Jenkins.

In the next chapter, we will explore Jenkins Extension Points, look at the theory behind them, and review the best practices of development.

5
Extension Points

In this chapter, we will introduce and explore the theory and design concepts used while developing Jenkins plugins. We will cover the high-level concepts here with some generic examples as a preparation for the next two chapters where we will see how to implement these ideas for real.

In this chapter, we will take a look at the following design patterns:

- Interfaces
- Abstract classes
- Singletons

Also, we will review several important design concepts:

- Design by contract
- Extension points
- Creating extensions
- Annotations

A brief history of Jenkins plugins

There are thousands of plugins available for Jenkins, and they cover a vast range of tasks and provide a wealth of valuable resources for the community that uses and works with Jenkins. Many of the existing plugins started out by providing simple functions and offering limited functionalities, but the majority of them have grown and developed into very mature software that offers large degrees of functionality. Many plugins have also been incorporated into Jenkins core functionality—turning them from an additional and optional add-on component to code that is shipped within Jenkins by default.

A major part of the reason for the success of Jenkins and its range of plugins is the design philosophy that was used to develop and extend Jenkins from the beginning. This approach to software development has encouraged people to work together, enabled projects to benefit from each other, and created a highly productive and collaborative community of developers and contributors to this project.

When you first look at developing your own plugin for Jenkins, there are several questions you should first address—the following link gives a detailed description of the steps you should take before embarking on developing your own new plugin:

```
https://wiki.jenkins-ci.org/display/JENKINS/
Before+starting+a+new+plugin
```

The intention behind this is to improve the quality of the plugins and to avoid duplication. This approach seeks to encourage developers of both existing and future or proposed plugins to work together and build upon the existing functionality rather than have a plethora of very similar plugins, all doing something slightly different.

If you are looking for some additional functionality that is not available in the current list of plugins, it is possible that someone might be working on providing this feature right now. If you publicize your requirements and intentions within the development community, this might save you a lot of time and trouble. Instead of rolling your own, you could instead offer to collaborate on the development of this new plugin. The end result of this collaboration is more likely to produce a popular and high-quality product than two developers creating a similar functionality. It's also possible that you will find a vast majority of the functionality that you are seeking already available within a related plugin, and with a little information and collaboration, you may be able to leverage this to add a new feature by reusing much of the existing code.

All of this collaboration, code reuse, and enhancement are achieved largely through the use of **Extension Points**, which represent some aspect of the functionality of either a plugin or of Jenkins. These are interfaces and abstract classes that enable interaction and reuse between different plugins and the Jenkins core functionality through declared and publicized entry points that provide and perform services to a documented contract.

We will now take a quick look at the theory behind these ideas so that when we write our own plugin, we will understand what is going on behind the scenes and why we are doing things with this reuse and extension in mind from the start.

Interfaces

Interfaces in Java are the mechanisms used to provide and declare a **contract** that defines how to interact with and reuse an existing software. The main idea behind this approach is that it removes the requirement of knowing how things are done internally; you only need to know what the required input parameters should be and what to expect by calling an interface. Exactly what the internal workings of the code are and how the processing is done are not really important, and as long as you adhere to the declared contract, everything should be ok.

Another major benefit of this "design by contract" approach is that it reduces the impact of code and process updates on external users. For example, if you call an `add` interface on a class called `calculator` that takes two numbers and returns the result, you (as a consumer of this service) do not need to know or care how the addition is done—internally, the class could be simply adding the two Java integers together, or perhaps the input variables are being passed over to a web service in the cloud somewhere, which returns the answer back to the `calculator`. The code and the approach used could be completely redesigned and rewritten in any way the developers of the `calculator` desire, but as long as everyone sticks to the agreed contract and interface, external consumers should not be affected.

This clearly-defined interface also makes it easier to write automated regression tests. When you know there is a clearly-defined and stable interface, it is usually simple to write tests against it that will not require much maintenance, as the interface is not normally likely to be changed. These tests can be automatically rerun as part of the CI build whenever there is a related code change, and any discrepancy should be easily identified.

To create an interface in Java, we use the **interface** keyword in the class definition:

```
interface Vehicle {
  // Vehicle methods
  // …
}
```

For an external class to use this interface, we use the **implements** keyword in the class declaration, as follows:

```
class Motorbike implements Vehicle {
  // Vehicle Methods
  // …
  // Motorbike Methods
  // …
}
```

As the `Motorbike` class has declared that it implements `Vehicle`, it will need to implement each of the methods that are declared in `Vehicle`. The Java compiler will ensure that this is done at compile time. For our `Vehicle` example, the methods would probably include logical functions, such as start, stop, turn left, turn right, brake, and accelerate. The `Motorbike` class-specific methods could include specifics, such as "pop a wheelie", extending the kickstand, falling over, and so forth.

Abstract classes

Abstract classes in Java provide a high-level functionality that can be used by other classes as well. You can't create an abstract class directly, but you can implement another class that derives from the abstract class.

The simplest explanation is that an abstract class is a type of a thing, but is not a thing — by this, I mean that you can have an abstract class like our `Vehicle` example that declares all of the methods that we mentioned, but you can't ever create just a vehicle — you have to have something specific, such as a car, motorbike, hovercraft, helicopter, and so on; you can't have just a generic vehicle.

All of our vehicles are slightly different, but share the same base functionality — they can go, they can stop, and they can turn. This common set of functionalities could, therefore, be modeled as base methods of an abstract (`Vehicle`) class, and whenever you create a new type of vehicle, you will have all of them available to you.

To create an abstract class in Java, you have to use the `abstract` keyword:

```
abstract class Vehicle{}
```

Typically, an abstract class will define the methods (go, stop, turn) only, and the subclasses will provide their actual implementation.

Our `Motorbike` class would then extend this abstract class:

```
class Motorbike extends Vehicle {}
```

The subclasses that extend the abstract classes are known as **concrete classes**:

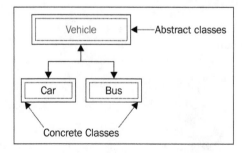

Unlike the conceptual and logical grouping of abstract classes, these represent real, tangible objects.

Abstraction and interfaces

Extension points make use of both abstraction and interfaces to permit and encourage reuse of functionality.

In the following diagram, **Deposit Money** declares an extension point called **Transfer to savings**. If we consider this to be an existing piece of code, and for the sake of this example, if we want to create a new **Savings Account** object, we can extend the functionality already provided by Deposit Money and use this to implement a new feature called Savings Account, which extends Deposit Money. This means that it will use most of the Deposit Money functionality, and it will also offer additional functionality of its own.

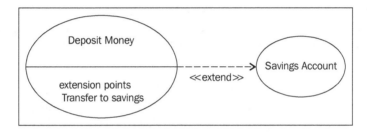

In another example, we are extending the existing `Open Account` code to `Add Joint Account Holder`. This uses many of the `Open Account` methods, but also declares some methods that are specific to a second applicant. The following diagram shows the relations:

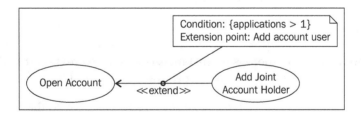

In cases where we have more than one application, we can extend Open Account to create a new **Add Joint Account Holder** object. This new object will contain and reuse a lot of the Open Account code, but it will do so slightly differently to cater to a secondary account holder.

Abstract types are a key concept in Java programming and in object-orientated design, in general. They are sometimes referred to as **existential** types, which help to reinforce what they are—*types of a thing* but without the required implementation or properties to actually be *a thing*.

Singletons

Before we move on from the high-level and design theory topic and take a look at implementing extensions in Jenkins, there is one more Java design pattern that we still need to cover—the Singleton pattern.

Singletons are used when you want to ensure that there will only be either zero or one instance of a given class.

Typically, this pattern occurs when you need to control concurrent actions—by ensuring that there is only a maximum of one instance possible, we can be sure that we will not face any concurrency or race conditions, as this class (and its code) will *definitely* be the only possible instance at any given time. Usually, a Singleton will be used by many different functions, and its purpose is to handle and manage this demand safely.

A common Singleton example is a logging utility. For example, a class that takes a message from several different areas of a system at any point in time. It then opens a log file and appends the message to the file. We wouldn't want two classes writing to the same log file at the same time—that would cause chaos and end horribly—so control and access is managed by and restricted to a maximum of one instance of the class. This instance will be guaranteed to have ownership and free rein to write to the log files, and it will be safe in the knowledge that there is no other instance of the same class doing the same thing at the same time—it manages the "write this information to the log file" function safely.

Each section of code that wishes to use the "write to log file" method will attempt to initialize the Singleton object. If an instance of this object already exists, we will reuse this, and if currently there is no instance, one will be created. It will then remain available for other users until the program exists, or it is cleaned up.

A Singleton instantiation is managed via a private constructor so that only the code inside the Singleton can create it, as follows:

```
public class Singleton {
    private static Singleton uniqueInstance = new Singleton();

    private Singleton() {}
```

```
    public static Singleton getInstance() {
      return uniqueInstance;
    }

    public String getDescription() {
      return "Singleton class";
    }
  }
```

This is known as Eager instantiation, as we will create a new Singleton object every time prior to invoking the getInstance() method.

The alternative approach to this—and which one you use depends on your preferences and requirements—is to use Lazy instantiation, as shown here:

```
public class Singleton {
  private static Singleton uniqueInstance;
  private Singleton() {}

  public static synchronized Singleton getInstance() {
    if (uniqueInstance == null) {
      uniqueInstance = new Singleton();
    }
    return uniqueInstance;
  }

  public String getDescription() {
    return "Singleton class";
  }
}
```

Here, we have used a static Singleton instance and synchronized the getInstance() method. Comparing the two approaches should help you to decide the best approach for your needs. In UML, a Singleton can be documented like this:

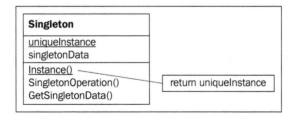

Declaring an extension in Jenkins

As we have seen so far, creating an interface or an abstract class is simple once we understand the logic behind them. It's easier to declare an interface or an abstract class, and then implement the required functionality.

Creating a Singleton is also straightforward once you understand when to use each design pattern and which approach suits your requirements.

If we keep this model in mind when creating or adding components to a Jenkins plugin, we should be able to identify appropriate opportunities where it would be helpful to expose an interface and create an extension point for others to use. For example, if you are working on a plugin that for some reason transforms the history of a Jenkins job in to a CSV file so that it can be exported and analyzed in a spreadsheet, you will be writing functions to turn some data in to CSV values—this could be declared as an extension point, and as long as the data passed is of the specified type, others can reuse your code to convert their data to CSV too, rather than everyone implementing the same functions, which would cause needless duplication.

To define or create an extension in Jenkins, we use the `@Extension` annotation type.

This annotation is picked up by Jenkins, and the new extension will be added to an `ExtensionList` object, where the extension can then be found via `ExtensionFinder`.

More details on the extension annotation can be found here: `http://javadoc.jenkins-ci.org/?hudson/Extension.html`.

The following example shows the declaration for an `Animal` extension point:

```
/**
 * Extension point that defines different kinds of animals
 */
public abstract class Animal implements ExtensionPoint {

  ...

  /**
   * All registered {@link Animal}s.
   */
  public static ExtensionList<Animal> all() {
    return Hudson.getInstance().getExtensionList(Animal.class);
  }
}
```

This illustrates an abstract class that implements `ExtensionPoint`: `https://wiki.jenkins-ci.org/display/JENKINS/Defining+a+new+extension+point`.

Summary

In this chapter, we looked at the concepts behind several major design patterns and saw when you would use each approach and why you would do so.

If you are an experienced Java programmer, these concepts should be very familiar, and if not, then hopefully this will serve as a foundation that will help you to understand not only what we are doing in the subsequent chapters, but also why we are doing it.

In the beginning of this chapter, we touched upon the philosophy behind plugin development—that people should seek to collaborate, reuse, and extend existing code to provide new functionality whenever possible. If everyone went off and created their own plugins for their own particular needs, rather than collaborating and contributing to existing efforts, there would be massive duplication and replication, and the quality would be far poorer as a result.

This ethos and the preceding design approach has created a community of plugin developers who produce high quality software by providing a vast array of functionality that enables Jenkins users to adapt and extend Jenkins to perform an incredibly diverse number of tasks.

In the next chapter, we will build upon this knowledge and see the concepts that we have covered here being used for real when we develop our first Jenkins plugin.

6
Developing Your Own Jenkins Plugin

In the previous chapter, we focused on the high-level concepts behind Jenkins plugins.

In this chapter, we will be hands-on as we work through the practical aspects of setting up our development environment, become familiar with the tools and conventions that we need to know about, and then create our first Jenkins plugin.

By the end of the chapter, you should be familiar with the following:

- Using Maven for builds and dependency management
- The structure and layout used for plugin projects
- Creating your own Jenkins plugin project(s)
- Making basic code changes to your plugin source code
- Compiling, packaging, and deploying your plugin to a remote Jenkins instance
- Using an IDE to make changes and run Jenkins
- The basics of running and debugging Jenkins and your plugin code within an IDE

We will begin by setting up our development environment; then, as is traditional, we will create a very simple `Hello World` Jenkins plugin project to illustrate the mechanics and get us started.

Most of this chapter is based on the topics covered in the Jenkins Plugin tutorial guide here:

```
https://wiki.jenkins-ci.org/display/JENKINS/Plugin+tutorial
```

This page has many useful references and should be your first port of call if you have any difficulty with any aspect of this chapter.

We will focus initially on the tools, conventions, and frameworks and keep to the simplest plugin possible to provide a solid understanding of the process and tools used to develop plugins. We will look at extension points and more complex code changes in the next chapter.

We will also run through the setting up of an IDE for plugin development and introduce basic Jenkins debugging that can be done directly from within Eclipse.

 To start off, we are concentrating on using Java and Maven as they are currently the most common tool set that are used to build plugins, but we will also take a look at alternative approaches such as Groovy and Gradle in the next chapter.

Let's start off by setting up your environment.

An introduction to Maven

We will use Maven to build our plugin. If you are unfamiliar with Maven, don't worry—the main point of Maven is that you don't necessarily need to know a lot about Maven to use it and to get a lot from it!

For a build tool that's quite unusual, you may well have expected yourself to be knee-deep in configuration files and code. However, Maven works quite well without these due to the core philosophy that is at its heart: it uses *convention over configuration*.

Maven works on the assumption that you and your project are following a set of standard, sensible conventions. These are nothing too weird or onerous, so if you are following this path, then Maven should just know where everything is and what you would like to achieve and will help you get up and running very quickly and easily.

One of these core assumptions is related to your project structure; specifically, if you are using a directory layout like this:

Item	Default dir (relative to the project directory)
source code	`src/main/java`
resources	`src/main/resources`
tests	`src/test`
complied code	`target`
distributable JAR	`target/classes`

Given a project that adheres to this convention, Maven will automatically know how to build your code, how to test it, and how to package it all up nicely for you with no other configuration or intervention required, providing a lot of benefit for a very small cost.

 This is great as long as your project sticks to the path that Maven expects… if you stray, things can get messy very quickly! This makes Maven great for new and well-structured projects, but requires a bit more work when introducing legacy projects that have their own ideas about locations and naming conventions.

Installing Maven

Maven is a Java tool, and therefore, we need to have Java installed to use it. You should have Java on your system already if you're running Jenkins locally, but if not, you can download a JDK for your platform from the following link—version 6.0 or later is required:

`http://www.oracle.com/technetwork/java/javase/downloads/index.html`

Once you've got the Java prerequisite sorted out, download Maven for your platform from the Apache site here:

`https://maven.apache.org/download.cgi`

Then follow the installation steps for your operating system from this page:

`https://maven.apache.org/install.html`

On all platforms, the main requirement is to ensure that you have a `JAVA_HOME` variable in `PATH`, and that `PATH` also contains the Maven `bin` directory from the download you extracted.

Once you are set up, you should get something roughly comparable to the following when you run `java -version` and then `mvn -version`—I am also displaying the Java and Maven environment variables here for your information:

```
MacDonald:~ donaldsimpson$ java -version
java version "1.8.0_51"
Java(TM) SE Runtime Environment (build 1.8.0_51-b16)
Java HotSpot(TM) 64-Bit Server VM (build 25.51-b03, mixed mode)
MacDonald:~ donaldsimpson$
MacDonald:~ donaldsimpson$ mvn -version
Apache Maven 3.3.3 (7994120775791599e205a5524ec3e0dfe41d4a06; 2015-04-22T12:57:37+01:00)
Maven home: /Users/donaldsimpson/Maven3
Java version: 1.8.0_51, vendor: Oracle Corporation
Java home: /Library/Java/JavaVirtualMachines/jdk1.8.0_51.jdk/Contents/Home/jre
Default locale: en_US, platform encoding: UTF-8
OS name: "mac os x", version: "10.10.4", arch: "x86_64", family: "mac"
MacDonald:~ donaldsimpson$
MacDonald:~ donaldsimpson$ set | grep _HOME
JAVA_HOME=/Library/Java/JavaVirtualMachines/jdk1.8.0_51.jdk/Contents/Home
M2_HOME=/Users/donaldsimpson/Maven3
MacDonald:~ donaldsimpson$ []
```

We now need to tell Maven about Jenkins; where it is and how to build it. We do this by updating the `settings.xml` file in the m2 home directory with the XML provided in the **Setting up Environment** section of the Jenkins Plugin Tutorial page mentioned earlier:

`https://wiki.jenkins-ci.org/display/JENKINS/Plugin+tutorial`

Find your `settings.xml` file here for Linux or Mac: `~/.m2/settings.xml`.

For Windows, the file is available at: `%USERPROFILE%\.m2\`.

Add the following text within the `settings.xml` file:

```
<settings>
  <pluginGroups>
    <pluginGroup>org.jenkins-ci.tools</pluginGroup>
  </pluginGroups>

  <profiles>
    <!-- Give access to Jenkins plugins -->
    <profile>
      <id>jenkins</id>
      <activation>
        <activeByDefault>true</activeByDefault>
```

```
        <!-- change this to false, if you don't like to have it
        on per default -->
      </activation>
      <repositories>
        <repository>
          <id>repo.jenkins-ci.org</id>
          <url>http://repo.jenkins-ci.org/public/</url>
        </repository>
      </repositories>
      <pluginRepositories>
        <pluginRepository>
          <id>repo.jenkins-ci.org</id>
          <url>http://repo.jenkins-ci.org/public/</url>
        </pluginRepository>
      </pluginRepositories>
    </profile>
  </profiles>
  <mirrors>
    <mirror>
      <id>repo.jenkins-ci.org</id>
      <url>http://repo.jenkins-ci.org/public/</url>
      <mirrorOf>m.g.o-public</mirrorOf>
    </mirror>
  </mirrors>
</settings>
```

It's a good idea to make a new directory for each project. This keeps things clean and simple, rather than having multiple projects coexist in one folder. To create a directory for this project, run `mkdir` and then `cd` to enter into the directory as follows:

```
mkdir jenkinspluginexample
cd jenkinspluginexample
```

After this, we can start the build, which will create a skeleton plugin project for us:

```
mvn -U org.jenkins-ci.tools:maven-hpi-plugin:create
```

If you have any issues at this point, check these three common causes first:

- Does `mvn` work in this directory? Check using `mvn -version`
- Does Java work in this directory? Check using `java -version`
- Do you have Internet connectivity? Check using `ping www.google.com`

If all goes well, you will be prompted to answer a couple of simple questions; Maven will want you to specify the `groupId` and the `artifactId` parameters of your plugin.

For `groupId`, the convention is to use your domain name in reverse followed by the project name, all in lower case and separated by dots. Given the `donaldsimpson.co.uk` domain name and the `jenkinspluginexample` project name, I would use this: `uk.co.donaldsimpson.jenkinspluginexample`.

The value of `artifactId` should be your project name, that is, `jenkinspluginexample`.

If you are going to have several components or services comprising the `jenkinspluginexample` project, you should append additional service names here, such as the following:

jenkinspluginexample-service

jenkinspluginexample-web

jenkinspluginexample-gui

The intention behind this approach is to ensure that when used in conjunction with the group ID, each part of your project will remain uniquely and readily identifiable.

```
1. bash
MacDonald:jenkinspluginexample donaldsimpson$ pwd
/Users/donaldsimpson/jenkinspluginexample
MacDonald:jenkinspluginexample donaldsimpson$ mvn -U org.jenkins-ci.tools:maven-hpi-plugin:create
[INFO] Scanning for projects...
Downloading: https://repo.maven.apache.org/maven2/org/jenkins-ci/tools/maven-hpi-plugin/maven-metadata.xml
Downloading: http://repo.jenkins-ci.org/public/org/jenkins-ci/tools/maven-hpi-plugin/maven-metadata.xml
Downloaded: http://repo.jenkins-ci.org/public/org/jenkins-ci/tools/maven-hpi-plugin/maven-metadata.xml (2 KB at 1.9 K
B/sec)
[INFO]
[INFO] ------------------------------------------------------------------------
[INFO] Building Maven Stub Project (No POM) 1
[INFO] ------------------------------------------------------------------------
[INFO]
[INFO]
[INFO] --- maven-hpi-plugin:1.114-cloudbees-1:create (default-cli) @ standalone-pom ---
Enter the groupId of your plugin [org.jenkins-ci.plugins]: uk.co.donaldsimpson.jenkinspluginexample
Enter the artifactId of your plugin (normally without '-plugin' suffix): jenkinspluginexample
[INFO] Defaulting package to group ID + artifact ID: uk.co.donaldsimpson.jenkinspluginexample.jenkinspluginexample
[INFO]
[INFO] Using following parameters for creating Archetype: maven-hpi-plugin:1.114-cloudbees-1
[INFO]
[INFO] Parameter: basedir, Value: /Users/donaldsimpson/jenkinspluginexample
[INFO] Parameter: package, Value: uk.co.donaldsimpson.jenkinspluginexample.jenkinspluginexample
[INFO] Parameter: groupId, Value: uk.co.donaldsimpson.jenkinspluginexample
[INFO] Parameter: artifactId, Value: jenkinspluginexample
[INFO] Parameter: version, Value: 1.0-SNAPSHOT
[INFO] ******************** End of debug info from resources from generated POM ************************
[INFO] Archetype created in dir: /Users/donaldsimpson/jenkinspluginexample/jenkinspluginexample
[INFO]
[INFO] ------------------------------------------------------------------------
[INFO] BUILD SUCCESS
[INFO] ------------------------------------------------------------------------
[INFO] Total time: 23.186 s
[INFO] Finished at: 2015-09-15T12:24:02+01:00
[INFO] Final Memory: 18M/236M
[INFO] ------------------------------------------------------------------------
MacDonald:jenkinspluginexample donaldsimpson$ []
```

The preceding screenshot is the result of the previous input and states that a version 1.0 Snapshot build has been created using the skeleton plugin, which has produced a very basic and the first plugin for us to examine.

Now take a look inside the newly created subdirectory, whose name should match your `artifactId`.

On exploring this directory, we should now have the generated examples of everything that is required to create the most basic plugin. These include the following:

- `pom.xml`: A new Maven POM file for our project that contains the information required for Maven to build, package, and distribute our example plugin
- `src/main`: This directory contains both a Java directory and a resources directory
- `src/main/java`: This directory contains the `Hello World` builder class that we will update later
- `src/main/resources`: This folder contains configuration and help files

Taking a good look around at the contents of these new folders that we just generated and mentioned will help you become familiar with the different files and structure used by Maven and Jenkins to develop, build, and distribute plugins. The layout follows the Maven conventions and is used for many other projects as well.

As you previously saw, our new project directory has its own `pom.xml` file, so we should be able to build it as a Maven project—let's take a look and try it out!

Change directory to the location of your new `pom.xml` file and have a look at it—you will see the various goals available in here, along with all of the details required to work with our project.

There is also a packaging declaration, as follows:

```
<packaging>hpi</packaging>
```

This tells Maven that you would like this project to be packaged into an HPI file—this is the standard file format for Jenkins plugins. Other packaging instructions typically include ZIP, JAR, WAR, and EAR.

Maven also assumes that you will want to perform a standard set of tasks with your project—these will usually include functions, or **phases** such as the following:

- `validate`: This validates that the project is correct and all necessary information is available.

- `compile`: This compiles the source code of the project.

- `test`: This tests the compiled source code using a suitable unit testing framework. The tests should not require the code be packaged or deployed.

- `package`: This takes the compiled code and packages it in its distributable format, such as a JAR.

- `integration-test`: This processes and deploys the package, if necessary, into an environment where integration tests can be run.

- `verify`: This runs checks to verify that the package is valid and meets quality criteria.

- `install`: This installs the package into the local repository, for use as a dependency in other projects locally.

- `deploy`: This is done in an integration or release environment. This function copies the final package to the remote repository to share the package with other developers and projects.

- `clean`: This cleans up artifacts created by prior builds.

- `site`: This generates site documentation for this project.

This guide has more information on Maven phases and goals and how they are linked:

```
https://maven.apache.org/guides/getting-started/maven-in-five-
minutes.html
```

If we run the `package` goal now, Maven should run through all of the prerequisite steps and then produce an HPI file, which we can deploy to Jenkins by running the following:

```
mvn package
```

This phase will download all the required dependencies using the information in the POM file. It will then compile the Java code and would also run tests (if any existed in the expected location—`src/test`).

Depending on your Internet connection, this may take some time, as Maven will perform an initial download for all the declared dependencies (and their dependencies!) that it doesn't already have locally. In subsequent runs, things should be much quicker, as Maven will retain the downloaded resources in the `.m2/repository` cache folder, which is in your home directory next to settings.xml that we updated earlier.

On completion, you should now have a distributable `.hpi` file!

```
1. bash
Downloaded: http://repo.jenkins-ci.org/public/org/apache/maven/maven-error-diagnostics/2.0/maven-error-diagnostics-2.
0.jar (11 KB at 7.5 KB/sec)
Downloading: http://repo.jenkins-ci.org/public/org/apache/maven/maven-artifact-manager/2.0/maven-artifact-manager-2.0
.jar
Downloaded: http://repo.jenkins-ci.org/public/org/apache/maven/maven-repository-metadata/2.0/maven-repository-metadat
a-2.0.jar (21 KB at 12.8 KB/sec)
Downloading: http://repo.jenkins-ci.org/public/org/apache/maven/maven-monitor/2.0/maven-monitor-2.0.jar
Downloading: http://repo.jenkins-ci.org/public/org/apache/maven/maven-plugin-registry/2.0/maven-plugin-registry-2.0.ja
r (25 KB at 15.3 KB/sec)
Downloading: http://repo.jenkins-ci.org/public/org/codehaus/groovy/groovy/1.6.5/groovy-1.6.5.jar
Downloaded: http://repo.jenkins-ci.org/public/org/codehaus/plexus/plexus-container-default/1.0-alpha-8/plexus-contain
er-default-1.0-alpha-8.jar (191 KB at 116.7 KB/sec)
Downloaded: http://repo.jenkins-ci.org/public/org/apache/maven/maven-project/2.0/maven-project-2.0.jar (103 KB at 56.
0 KB/sec)
Downloaded: http://repo.jenkins-ci.org/public/org/apache/maven/maven-monitor/2.0/maven-monitor-2.0.jar (8 KB at 3.8 K
B/sec)
Downloaded: http://repo.jenkins-ci.org/public/org/apache/maven/maven-artifact-manager/2.0/maven-artifact-manager-2.0.
jar (50 KB at 24.7 KB/sec)
Downloaded: http://repo.jenkins-ci.org/public/org/codehaus/groovy/groovy/1.6.5/groovy-1.6.5.jar (3872 KB at 527.7 KB/
sec)
[INFO] Generated /Users/donaldsimpson/jenkinspluginexample/jenkinspluginexample/target/jenkinspluginexample/WEB-INF/l
icenses.xml
[INFO]
[INFO] --- maven-hpi-plugin:1.106:hpi (default-hpi) @ jenkinspluginexample ---
[INFO] Generating /Users/donaldsimpson/jenkinspluginexample/jenkinspluginexample/target/jenkinspluginexample/META-INF
/MANIFEST.MF
[INFO] Building jar: /Users/donaldsimpson/jenkinspluginexample/jenkinspluginexample/target/jenkinspluginexample.jar
[INFO] Exploding webapp...
[INFO] Copy webapp webResources to /Users/donaldsimpson/jenkinspluginexample/jenkinspluginexample/target/jenkinsplugi
nexample
[INFO] Assembling webapp jenkinspluginexample in /Users/donaldsimpson/jenkinspluginexample/jenkinspluginexample/targe
t/jenkinspluginexample
[INFO] Generating hpi /Users/donaldsimpson/jenkinspluginexample/jenkinspluginexample/target/jenkinspluginexample.hpi
[INFO] Building jar: /Users/donaldsimpson/jenkinspluginexample/jenkinspluginexample/target/jenkinspluginexample.hpi
[INFO] ------------------------------------------------------------------------
[INFO] BUILD SUCCESS
[INFO] ------------------------------------------------------------------------
[INFO] Total time: 08:40 min
[INFO] Finished at: 2015-09-15T13:00:13+01:00
[INFO] Final Memory: 49M/414M
[INFO] ------------------------------------------------------------------------
MacDonald:jenkinspluginexample donaldsimpson$ []
```

As you can see from the preceding image, the console output that is produced near the end explains that the code has been compiled into a Java Archive (`.jar`) file, the resources (the Jelly, configuration, and HTML files) have been included, and everything has, in my case, been packaged into a resultant archive named `jenkinspluginexample.hpi`, which now resides in the `target/` directory.

We haven't written a line of code yet, but we have just produced our first Jenkins plugin!

Let's now deploy this to a standard Jenkins instance:

1. Open the home page for your Jenkins instance.
2. Navigate to Jenkins **Home | Manage Jenkins**.
3. Select **Manage Plugins**, and then **Advanced**.
4. Scroll down to the **Upload Plugin** section and click on **Browse**.
5. Navigate to the local folder where your new `.hpi` file is (in the target directory of your project):

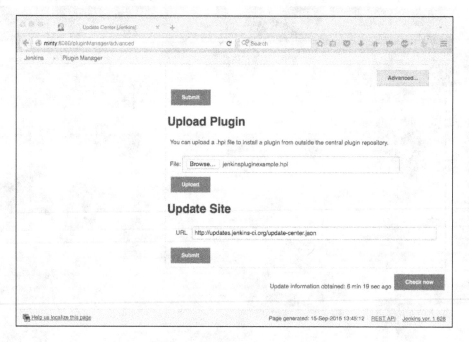

After clicking the **Submit** button, you should see that your plugin is uploaded and installed on your Jenkins instance:

You will now have a TODO plugin in your list of installed plugins, along with the Snapshot build number and your name as the author.

If you now click on **Configure** of any Freestyle job, there will be a new option to add a build step called **Say hello world**:

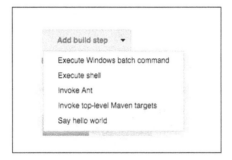

Selecting this will produce the following dialog, where you supply your name:

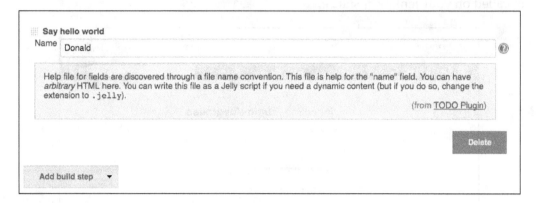

Not too surprisingly, for a `Hello World` project, this will be displayed as an additional build step in the console output the next time you run this job:

It looks pretty cool to have our own plugin installed and running on a Jenkins instance, and doing this for the first time is good fun. However, when you are developing a plugin, running through a process like this every time you make a small change is a bit more of a hassle than you may want!

Let's now look at making our first code change and a smarter and more efficient way to package, deploy, and test our code.

To start off with, make a tiny change as follows to the `HelloWorldBuilder.java` file, which is in your `src/main/java` directory:

```
src/main/java/uk/co/donaldsimpson/jenkinspluginexample/
jenkinspluginexample/HelloWorldBuilder.java
```

```
public class HelloWorldBuilder extends Builder {

    private final String name;

    // Fields in config.jelly must match the parameter names in the "DataBoundConstructor"
    @DataBoundConstructor
    public HelloWorldBuilder(String name) {
        this.name = name;
    }

    /**
     * We'll use this from the <tt>config.jelly</tt>.
     */
    public String getName() {
        return name;
    }

    @Override
    public boolean perform(AbstractBuild build, Launcher launcher, BuildListener listener) {
        // This is where you 'build' the project.
        // Since this is a dummy, we just say 'hello world' and call that a build.

        // This also shows how you can consult the global configuration of the builder
        if (getDescriptor().getUseFrench())
            listener.getLogger().println("Bonjour, "+name+"!");
        else
            listener.getLogger().println("Hello there, "+name+"!");
        return true;
    }

    // Overridden for better type safety.
    // If your plugin doesn't really define any property on Descriptor,
    // you don't have to do this.
    @Override
    public DescriptorImpl getDescriptor() {
        return (DescriptorImpl)super.getDescriptor();
    }
}
```

Initially, the line was this:

```
listener.getLogger().println("Hello, "+name+"!");
```

I have simply altered the preceding line to the following:

```
listener.getLogger().println("Hello there, "+name+"!");
```

Instead of going all the way through the previous process again—compiling, packaging, and deploying through the Jenkins web page and so on—just to check this minor update, we can perform all these steps with one simple Maven command:

mvn hpi:run

This will compile the code (after picking up our modification), and then start up and run a local instance of Jenkins on your machine with our newly updated plugin already deployed to it—this makes the testing of your changes much easier, quicker, and safer too.

To do this on Windows, first export the following settings:

```
set MAVEN_OPTS=-Xdebug -Xrunjdwp:transport=dt_socket,server=y,address=800
0,suspend=n
```

On Unix and Mac, do the equivalent, as follows:

```
export MAVEN_OPTS="-Xdebug -Xrunjdwp:transport=dt_socket,server=y,address
=8000,suspend=n"
```

Then, regardless of platform, call the `hpi:run` goal, as shown here:

```
mvn hpi:run
```

After this, you will be able to see Maven download dependencies and then start up a local Jetty instance that runs Jenkins with your plugin installed on it!

Keep an eye on your console output, and you will see when everything is complete whenever the following text is displayed: **INFO: Jenkins is fully up and running**.

After this point, you can safely connect to the Jenkins instance by pointing your browser to the following:

```
http://127.0.0.1:8080/jenkins/
```

> Do not try to connect to the 8000 port you have set in MAVEN_OPTS — this is used for debugging, which we will take a look at later. Use port 8080, and note that the appended /jenkins/ path is also required in order to connect.

Now, we can create and configure a new Freestyle job and add in the same build step as before by selecting to use our **Say hello world** job and adding our name to it.

Running this new job should produce the expected output, as follows:

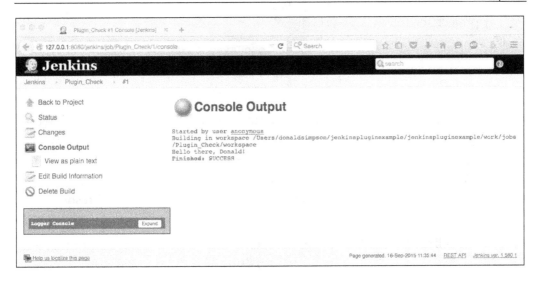

This proves that our code change has been picked up and demonstrates just how quickly and easily you can make, test, package, deploy, and verify your plugin changes—one small Maven command does most of the work for you! After the initial setup and downloading, it's a fairly quick process too.

To make life even easier, we can set up an IDE to help us develop Jenkins plugins.

> The official Jenkins Plugin Tutorial page is at `https://wiki.jenkins-ci.org/display/JENKINS/Plugin+tutorial`. This tutorial contains steps for NetBeans, IntelliJ IDEA, and Eclipse. The first two are very simple, so we'll cover the Eclipse setup in more detail here.

The plugin guide currently recommends using this command to generate a new Eclipse workspace for plugin development:

```
mvn -DdownloadSources=true -DdownloadJavadocs=true
  -DoutputDirectory=target/eclipse-classes -Declipse.workspace=
    /path/to/workspace eclipse:eclipse eclipse:add-maven-repo
```

You need to update `/path/to/workspace` to point to a suitable workspace location on your system—this can be anywhere you like, but ideally, next to your other Eclipse workspace(s).

> I had issues running the suggested command and found that `eclipse:add-maven-repo` is deprecated, so I updated this to `eclipse:configure-workspace` instead.

For my project, the following worked:

```
mvn -DdownloadSources=true -DdownloadJavadocs=true
  -DoutputDirectory=target/eclipse-classes -Declipse.workspace=
    /Users/donaldsimpson/Documents/JenkinsPluginEclipseWorkspace
        eclipse:eclipse eclipse:configure-workspace
```

Make sure you run this command from within the same directory that you have used to create the `Hello World` plugin, as it requires the `pom.xml` file and other resources from here.

On completion, this step should successfully populate a new Eclipse `.metadata` directory in your new workspace and have all the required settings and resources in your project directory.

Next, open Eclipse and switch to your chosen workspace, select **Import** (under the **File** menu), select **General** and then **Existing Projects into Workspace**, as follows:

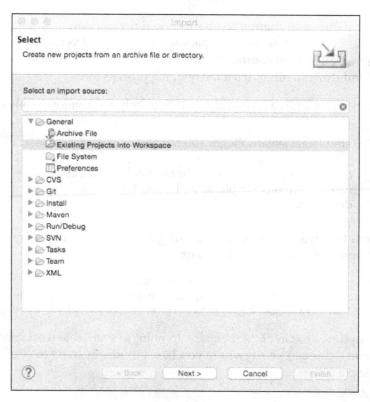

Direct this dialog to the directory where you created your Hello World plugin (where the pom.xml file is), and Eclipse should automatically load up the project for you:

On completion, you should have an IDE that looks something like this:

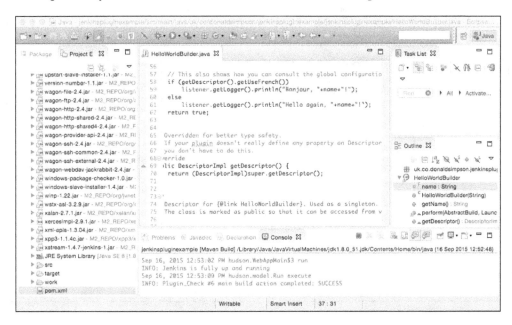

Now you can edit the Java classes and the plugin resources from within Eclipse.

 Remember that you can also enable the Mylyn plugin that we set up earlier to keep an eye on how your most important Jenkins builds are doing!

You can also manage your project's POM file and run the Maven build from here too—right-click on the `pom.xml` file and select **Run as** and **Maven Build**, and Jenkins should start up directly in your Eclipse console now, with your plugin already deployed with the latest version of your code.

To test this setup, try making another very simple change—in the preceding image, I updated the output message to **Hello again**, just to be different. Saving the `Hello World` builder class and then running the Maven target `hpi:run` through Eclipse will fire up Jenkins, and you can see the alteration made in Eclipse.

You can also run Jenkins in the **Debug** mode and set a breakpoint by clicking on the desired line of your code in Eclipse, as follows:

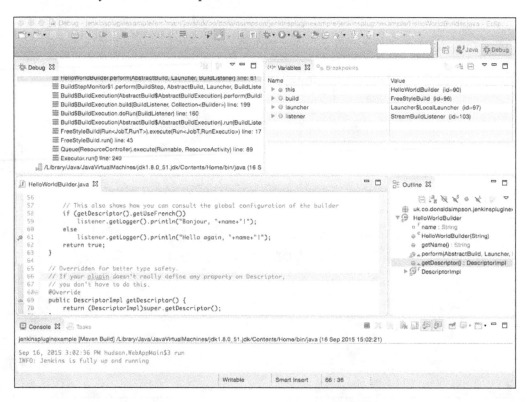

Here, we can see the breakpoint being activated when the build is run via Jenkins. At this point, the focus will automatically switch from Jenkins in the browser to the Eclipse IDE, where we can inspect the current values of the existing variables at run time. We can then walk through the code step by step by debugging the values in real time and monitoring the console output at each step.

This is a very handy development feature, and setting up your Jenkins plugin development environment in this manner can make things much more productive—and your life a lot easier!

Summary

In this chapter, we have built, packaged, and deployed our own "bare-bones" Jenkins plugin.

We have looked at the tools and conventions used to develop Jenkins plugins. We have set up Java, Maven, and Eclipse on our development host and learned how to build, package, test, deploy, and even debug our own plugin.

The main thing that we are still missing is what you decide to put in the middle! This is what we will concentrate on in the next chapter.

7
Extending Jenkins Plugins

For Jenkins plugin development so far, we have looked at the following:

- The approach to take—reuse where possible, avoiding unnecessary duplication
- Collaborating—how both the process and the community work
- Design methodologies and Java patterns used
- Setting up the development environment and build tools
- Developing the first simple plugin
- Deploying and testing our plugins locally and remotely

We will now take a look at the ways to help you sort out that missing middle part from the previous chapter and implement the code that enables your plugin to do what it does… whatever that may be!

The intention here is to walk you through the development of your own plugin and demonstrate the ways in which you can (and should) approach the (re)use of the resources that are already out there.

This means that when you come up with an idea for your own plugin and want to develop it, you will be able to do so as quickly and easily as possible by following best practices and by avoiding the addition of unnecessary duplication to the Jenkins and plugin code base.

While doing this, we will also explore some of the additional frameworks and technologies used by and available to Jenkins plugins. These include Jelly, Stapler, localization, and internationalization; when used together, these tools and practices enable plugin developers to reuse the Jenkins built-in functionality in order to make their plugins look like they "belong" to Jenkins, rather than something that has been simply added on, by maintaining the same look and feel as the rest of the user interface.

Following this approach of getting yourself started and knowing how to use these frameworks will save you a lot of time and frustration. Once you know how to go about researching and reusing the code and functionality that's already provided by the existing plugins and Jenkins, you will save yourself a lot of development work as well.

While working on the `Hello World` plugin, we covered quite a lot of new information and introduced some new concepts. This was all done at a pretty high level and with minimum coding and configuration so that we could maintain focus on the overall process and learn how things work. The actual code was about as simple as you can get for a plugin; all it did was write a message to the console log every time the build was run.

As you're no doubt aware, Jenkins plugins have been created to perform all kinds of tasks, and they do so in a wide variety of ways—some of them integrate seamlessly with the Jenkins user interface, while others work away mostly unseen in the background. Some extend existing functionalities and others add entirely new functions. Plugins seem to be cohesive—they all have roughly the same look and feel, rather than appear to have been developed by different people, who had their own ideas about color schemes, navigation, dialogs, and so on. They are even able to respond to locale changes to provide dialogs in different languages depending on user-specified preferences. While much of Jenkins functionality comes from a large number of plugins, many of which have been assimilated into the core of Jenkins, the impression and user experience is that of a quite slick and cohesive whole, rather than a collection of fragmented and disparate additions.

In this chapter, we will take a look at the other elements that go into Jenkins plugins, and expand the ways in which you can flesh out your own plugin. We will also look at how to go about finding and reusing existing code/plugins to get you started quickly, and we will walk through the contents of a plugin that offers features similar to a hypothetical new plugin that we would like to start developing.

Where to start?

So, after checking the Jenkins site and the community, we have decided to write a new plugin, as nothing out there (or currently in the works) will do whatever it is we want; where do we start?

We could start off with a new blank Eclipse project and write everything ourselves if we really wanted to, but that would take ages.

We could use the skeleton `Hello World` project, delete what is in there, and start adding our code to that, but this doesn't sound like the sort of approach we'd expect to follow, given all the code reuse and avoidance of duplication we've been talking about for a while now.

Even if you have a completely novel idea for a plugin, there is bound to be something roughly related to it out there already; even if this doesn't provide the functionality that we want, it may work in a similar way or use many of the same extension points that we have identified as being of interest to us, so it's worth checking this out.

Looking at the list of existing plugins

Usually, the first place to look at is the list of available plugins. If your Jenkins instance is up to date, you can browse through the currently available options in your Jenkins **Available plugins** page.

Go to **Manage Jenkins**, then select **Manage Plugins**, and select the **Available** tab for an ever-growing list of plugins to choose from.

Note that this screen allows you to filter by specific words and provides a brief description of each plugin.

Alternatively, the Jenkins **Plugins** page provides an easier-to-browse and slightly more detailed listing:

```
https://wiki.jenkins-ci.org/display/JENKINS/Plugins
```

This lists the plugins grouped by their general category or function and also hosts links to the corresponding Jenkins home page for each plugin. In turn, the home page provides further information that includes links to the source code for that plugin on GitHub, which you can browse online or download locally.

If you are able to find something similar to your plugin here, then going through the source code on GitHub will enable you to see how each plugin works in detail. You will also be able to find out what extension points this plugin uses.

Another option to consider is going straight to the **Extension points** index page here:

```
https://wiki.jenkins-ci.org/display/JENKINS/Extension+points
```

This list is automatically generated and maintained by the **Extension Indexer** program, which is available at:

```
https://github.com/jenkinsci/backend-extension-indexer
```

This program parses the current code base for all the declared extension points and then lists them on the **Extension points** page that it generates, along with further details such as the project home page and a list of the plugins that use them.

Whichever starting point works for you, the list of plugins or the list of extension points, you should hopefully end up at the same place—with an idea of something roughly similar to what you want to end up with, which should be a good place to get you started.

For example, if my plugin was connected to Docker, I could start searching through the list of existing plugins from here on my local Jenkins:

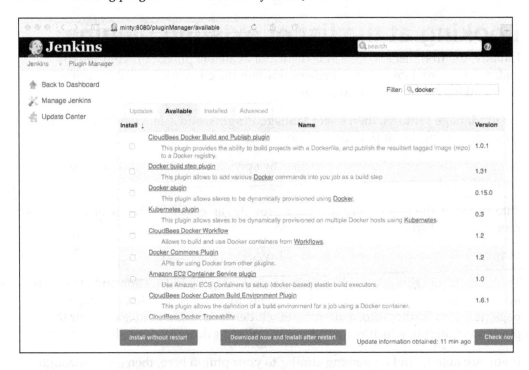

Alternatively, I could go to `https://wiki.jenkins-ci.org/display/JENKINS/Extension+points`, and search for Docker references here:

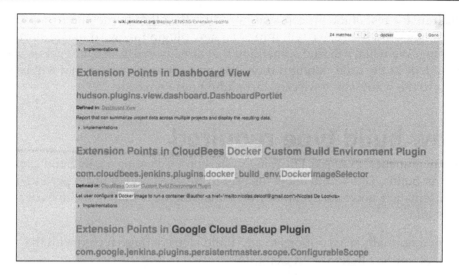

Both of these routes eventually lead to the home page of the plugin in question, for example:

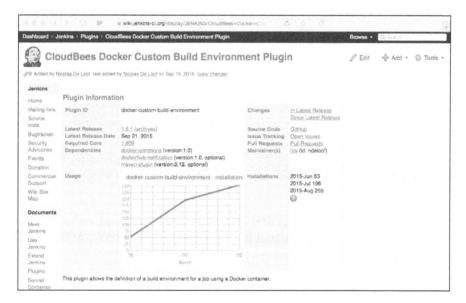

This tells you everything that you need to know about the plugin and includes a link to the source code and configuration files for this plugin that are hosted on GitHub.

To illustrate the rest of the process and introduce the other frameworks and files that you may want to use, we will think of a new plugin that we'd like to start developing. We will try to find something that already exists, use it to get us started, and then look at the code, configuration files, and extension points that will be used to get us to the point where we can start adding our own code.

A new build type required

For this hypothetical example, I'm going to start off by creating a new build step for Docker builds. This would allow the user to create a build of this type, add in some information, and then eventually do something with it along the lines of a Docker build.

Where you normally have options to add build steps of these types (with the addition of our **Say hello world** example):

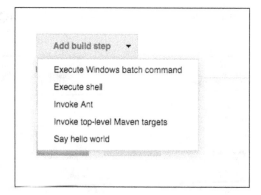

This amazing new plugin-to-be will add an additional entry to kick off a Docker Build.

By looking through similar projects that add additional build steps and from the `Hello World` example, I can guess that my new plugin will also want to extend the `Builder`, `BuildStep`, and `AbstractProject` classes.

After looking through the links and resources previously listed, I can see that there is an existing Graven Plugin project that performs very similar steps to what we are after and also just happens to include all of the new resources that we wanted to examine in this chapter. Plus, it's got some handy documentation here:

```
https://wiki.jenkins-ci.org/display/JENKINS/Create+a+new+Plugin+with+
a+custom+build+Step
```

Let's take a look at it. The source code can be downloaded from GitHub here and then extracted to a local directory:

```
https://github.com/jenkinsci/graven-plugin
```

This gives us everything we need to get started on our own plugin, which should make things much easier than starting from scratch—we can examine and reuse the extension points used here to see how the plugin goes about creating a new build type, and adjusts the properties files and other resources, as they perform the same steps that we want to do.

Loading and building our starting point

Let's import this project in to Eclipse. Again, the process is quite simple; as we did in the previous chapter, we will make a directory for our Eclipse Project, use cd to enter into the directory containing our project's POM file, and then run the eclipse:configure-workspace goal again, as follows:

```
mvn -DdownloadSources=true -DdownloadJavadocs=true
-DoutputDirectory=target/eclipse-classes -Declipse.workspace=
/Users/donaldsimpson/Documents/GravenPluginMasterWorkspace
eclipse:eclipse eclipse:configure-workspace
```

This should download all the dependencies and allow you to import the project to your IDE (navigate to **File | Import | General | Existing Projects in to Workspace**), in the same way as we did in the previous chapter.

You should now have all the resources and source code, which constitutes this plugin, loaded in to your IDE, and it should look roughly like this:

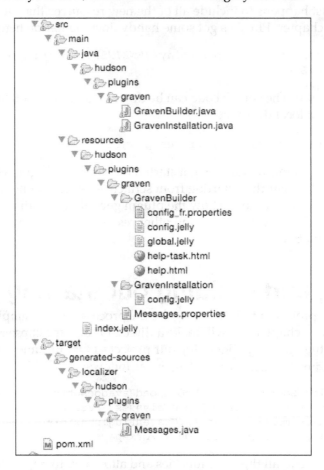

We will now take a quick look through these files and file types, explain their functions, and explore the additional plugin components and options they provide for this plugin, and could potentially bring to our new plugin.

The Builder class and Stapler

The first class is `GravenBuilder.java`. The class declares that it extends the `Builder` class:

```
public class GravenBuilder extends Builder {
```

As we can see in the JavaDoc at `http://javadoc.jenkins-ci.org/hudson/tasks/ Builder.html`, extending the `Builder` class will register this class with Jenkins as a **custom builder**, which is what we are after.

 This extension declaration is how the **Extension point** page is updated—the program that builds the index will find this reference in the code and automatically create the association for us.

The `GravenBuilder` class also contains this simple method:

```
@DataBoundConstructor
public GravenBuilder(String task) {
  this.task = task;
}
```

Through the use of the `@DataBoundConstructor` annotation, this method will register the selection of this task/build type when the user decides to create this new build type. This is done automatically via the Stapler framework, which Jenkins uses to serialize and convert Java objects. You can find out more about Stapler, how it works, and how to make use of it in your plugins here:

`http://stapler.kohsuke.org/what-is.html`

Also, in the `GravenBuilder` class, there is an inner class named `Descriptor`. This extends `BuildStepDescriptor`, and its function is to provide a way for Jenkins to manage instances of `GravenBuilder` and their lifecycles.

The `GravenInstallation` class contains all the required installation and registration settings; this sets the tool tips and defines the display name to be used for this plugin, and so on.

Jelly and Jenkins

The `config.jelly` configuration file is a simple Jelly template. You can find out more about Jelly in Jenkins in the following link:

`https://wiki.jenkins-ci.org/display/JENKINS/Basic+guide+to+Jelly+usag e+in+Jenkins`

You can read more about Jelly, in general, here at `http://commons.apache.org/proper/commons-jelly/`. This article states the following:

> *Jelly is a Java and XML based scripting and processing engine.*

The main purpose of Jelly in this context is to provide developers with a highly flexible tag library through which they can quickly and easily create and handle UI view changes.

From a developer point of view, Jelly files interact with Java code to get and set declared values at runtime and presents them to the user via the UI.

Help

The `help*.html` files provide context-sensitive help messages to the user. These messages are simply defined within the `<div>` tags and will be displayed as standard-looking tooltips within the Jenkins user interface. This approach allows you to guide your user, advise them on what they can and can't do, and explain what your plugin does and requires.

The `index.jelly` file provides the user with a general high-level description of what this plugin does—we will see this text being displayed as the plugin description in Jenkins when we look at the plugin in action later on.

Properties files and Messages

The `Messages.properties` and `config_fr.properties` files are there to provide users with i18n internationalization, as described here:

`https://wiki.jenkins-ci.org/display/JENKINS/Internationalization`

There is some more detail on localization and internationalization at this link:

`http://www.w3.org/International/questions/qa-i18n`

In Jenkins plugin development, all we really need to do is provide `config_LOCALE.properties` files to cater to each language. For example, if the user's `LOCALE` variable is set to `fr`, the messages in the `config_fr.properties` file will be used—other `LOCALE` files can be added as desired to support other languages.

Your plugin code is able to use and refer to the properties at runtime, as follows:

```
Messages.GravenBuilder_Task()
```

The `Messages.java` class in the target directory is generated at build time, based on these properties files.

The POM file

The last remaining file, `pom.xml`, is the Maven settings file that we have looked at before. This one is particular to the plugin we are using here and contains the group, artifact, and version information that will be used to build, run, and package the project, which we will do now.

Right-clicking on the `pom.xml` file and selecting **Run as** and then **Maven Build…** allows you to specify the `hpi:run` goal again, which should start up a new local instance of Jenkins with this plugin compiled and deployed to this new instance, along with all of the resources and localization settings the plugin contains.

When the instance starts up, we can connect via a browser and see the various settings and code that we have reviewed in theory being used in practice.

We can check and see that the plugin is listed as installed, along with the message text, which is picked up from `index.jelly`:

When we create a new Freestyle job and take a look at the available **Build** steps that we could add, this plugin will be displayed as a new option — **execute GRaveN task**, which has been picked up from **Messages.properties**:

When we select this option, we will be presented with the dialogs, localized tool tips, and input boxes that were defined in the configuration and code we just reviewed:

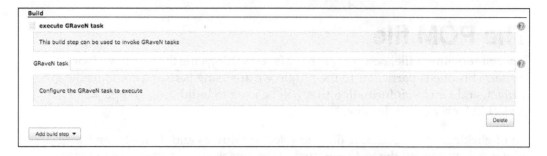

This example plugin looks like a good starting point for our hypothetical one. It may not do everything that we want to do, but we can adjust and reuse the settings files and some of the code and extension points it uses to get us started, and we can have the basics of our own plugin up and running very quickly.

The implementation of this hypothetical plugin, or your own plugin, may well have different needs when you get down to the details, but hopefully, this will illustrate the approaches and routes you could follow to get your plugin up and running quickly.

If you ever want to find out how a plugin works, or how to change a plugin, or fix a bug in a plugin, knowing your way around the various resource files and how to load and run any locally based plugin by starting off with its source code is a very useful skill.

Plugin progress

We searched and identified something that did roughly what we wanted to do, at least to start off with. We have identified extension points that provide some of the functionalities that we are after, and we have the beginnings of a pretty fully-featured plugin that will look and feel like a normal part of Jenkins. It will provide the user with inbuilt help and will even speak the user's preferred language... so long as we add the corresponding config files.

Summary

The next steps for this plugin would be to implement more of our own code, to perform the Docker build, or whatever functions we want to perform. Again, this functionality could take further advantage of the available extension points, or if there are none available that will do what we want, we should consider declaring their interfaces and sharing them with the community after coding our own implementation.

In the next chapter, we will explore the tools, options, and resources available for testing our plugins. We will also look further into debugging as we explore how to approach, resolve, and avoid issues with plugins.

8

Testing and Debugging Jenkins Plugins

In this chapter, we will take a look at the testing and debugging of Jenkins plugins. We will explore several popular options and approaches that are currently available, and we will review the benefits and suitability of each approach.

Testing Jenkins plugins is reasonably straightforward if you are happy to simply run standard Java Unit tests, but if you wish to test and mimic interactions via the user interface, testing can become a little bit more involved. We will start off with a simple example and then look at some of the approaches and tools you may want to investigate further for more complex scenarios.

Being able to debug a Jenkins plugins is a valuable addition to your development skills—it can help you understand what is going on with your own plugin while you are developing it, and it can also help you to resolve issues in other plugins or Jenkins itself.

In this chapter, we will take a look at the following topics:

- Testing: Under Testing, we'll cover the following topics:
    - Running tests for an existing project
    - Writing your own tests
    - Available tools
    - Techniques—HTML scraping, Mocking, and so on

- Debugging: Under Debugging, we'll cover the following topics:

    ◦ Standard log files

    ◦ Using the local Jenkins debug session

    ◦ Connecting from an IDE

    ◦ The `mvnDebug` command

Running tests with Maven

When we were exploring plugin development earlier, we learned where to find and how to fetch the source code for any given Jenkins plugin.

The full source code for most plugins can be quickly and easily downloaded from GitHub and then built on your local machine. In many cases, this also includes Unit tests, which are bundled with the source code and can be found in the expected (by Maven convention) location of `src/test`. Examining a selection of popular plugins would provide you with useful information and a great starting point to write your own test cases.

The Maven `test` target will execute all of the tests and produce a summary of the outcome by detailing all the usual statistics such as the number of tests run along with how many failures and errors there were and the number of skipped tests.

To demonstrate this process, we will take a look at the very popular `Green Balls` plugin, which simply replaces the standard blue balls in Jenkins with green ones.

 This link explains why Jenkins has blue balls as default:
`http://jenkins-ci.org/content/why-does-jenkins-have-blue-balls`

The Green Balls plugin homepage links to this GitHub location, where you can download the source and configuration files in a zip file or clone it using the URL provided:

`https://github.com/jenkinsci/greenballs-plugin`

We're looking at this example plugin, as it contains a good variety of tests that cover the main topics and styles of testing—we will take a closer look at the contents shortly. Once you have the source code downloaded to your local machine, you should be able to kick off the tests by simply running the Maven `test` target:

```
mvn test
```

This target will then run through all the prerequisite setup steps before executing all the tests and then report on the outcome as follows:

```
Oct 15, 2015 5:08:11 PM hudson.PluginWrapper stop
INFO: Stopping translation
Oct 15, 2015 5:08:11 PM hudson.PluginWrapper stop
INFO: Stopping ui-samples-plugin
Tests run: 4, Failures: 0, Errors: 0, Skipped: 0, Time elapsed: 2.14 sec

Results :

Tests run: 9, Failures: 0, Errors: 0, Skipped: 0

[INFO] ------------------------------------------------------------
[INFO] BUILD SUCCESS
[INFO] ------------------------------------------------------------
[INFO] Total time: 13.965 s
[INFO] Finished at: 2015-10-15T17:08:11+01:00
[INFO] Final Memory: 25M/542M
[INFO] ------------------------------------------------------------
MacDonald:greenballs-plugin-master donaldsimpson$ []
```

Note that a single test can be run by specifying the name of the test, as shown here:

```
mvn test -Dtest=GreenBallIntegrationTest
```

This will result in one test being run, or you can use wildcards such as this:

```
mvn test -Dtest=*ilter*
```

The preceding code results in four tests being run in this case.

This approach could be used to categorize your tests into logical suites — integration tests, nightly tests, regression tests, or unit tests — whatever you like, simply by applying a consistent naming convention to your test classes and then setting up Jenkins jobs, or running Maven targets that will perform the corresponding actions, for example:

```
mvn test -Dtest=*Integration*
```

The Green Balls plugin contains two test classes: GreenBallFilterTest and GreenBallIntegrationTest, which illustrate two different approaches of plugin testing — taking a look through their source code should help you to see how you can develop your own tests.

`GreenBallFilterTest` performs some simple pattern matching tests to ensure that correct images are in place:

```
import static org.hamcrest.CoreMatchers.equalTo;
import static org.hamcrest.CoreMatchers.is;
import static org.junit.Assert.assertThat;

import java.util.regex.Matcher;

import org.junit.Before;
import org.junit.Test;

public class GreenBallFilterTest {

  GreenBallFilter greenBallFilter;

  @Before
  public void setup() {
    greenBallFilter = new GreenBallFilter();
  }

  @Test
  public void patternShouldMatch() {
    final Matcher m = greenBallFilter.patternBlue.matcher("/nocacheImages/48x48/blue.gif");
    assertThat(m.find(), is(true));
    assertThat(m.group(1), equalTo("48x48"));
    assertThat(m.group(2), equalTo(""));
    assertThat(m.group(3), equalTo("gif"));
  }

  @Test
  public void patternShouldMatchPNG() {
    final Matcher m = greenBallFilter.patternBlue.matcher("/nocacheImages/48x48/blue.png");
    assertThat(m.find(), is(true));
    assertThat(m.group(1), equalTo("48x48"));
    assertThat(m.group(2), equalTo(""));
    assertThat(m.group(3), equalTo("png"));
  }
}
```

`GreenBallIntegrationTest`, as shown in the following screenshot, extends `HudsonTestCase` and uses `com.gargoylesoftware.htmlunit.WebResponse` to test and interact directly with the deployed web components, asserting that they return the expected results:

```
package hudson.plugins.greenballs;

import java.math.BigInteger;
import java.net.URL;
import java.security.MessageDigest;
import java.security.NoSuchAlgorithmException;
import java.util.Date;

import org.apache.commons.httpclient.util.DateUtil;
import org.jvnet.hudson.test.HudsonTestCase;

import com.gargoylesoftware.htmlunit.WebResponse;

/**
 *
 * @author Asgeir S. Nilsen
 */
public class GreenBallIntegrationTest extends HudsonTestCase {

    static String join(String first, String second) {
        if (first.endsWith("/"))
            first = first.substring(0, first.length() - 1);
        if (second.startsWith("/"))
            second = second.substring(1);
        return first + "/" + second;
    }

    static String hash(String algorithm, byte[] data) throws NoSuchAlgorithmException {
        byte[] hash = MessageDigest.getInstance(algorithm).digest(data);
        BigInteger bi = new BigInteger(1, hash);
        String result = bi.toString(16);
        if (result.length() % 2 != 0) {
            return "0" + result;
        }
        return result;
    }
```

This Jenkins page provides useful resources for further reading that would cater to more detailed and complex testing scenarios:

`https://wiki.jenkins-ci.org/display/JENKINS/Unit+Test`

This link covers topics such as Mocking, HTML scraping, submitting forms, JavaScript, and web page assertions.

Debugging Jenkins

The remainder of this chapter focuses on debugging in a number of different ways in order to help in further understanding the application and its behavior at run time.

The main focus is on using a local instance of Jenkins and an IDE to debug development sessions; however, it is still useful to know about the options available through the inbuilt logging options in Jenkins, which are sophisticated and highly customizable. These are often a good starting point for any kind of issue, so we will start with a quick overview of the options here before moving on to the type of debugging that you'll probably want to set up and use when developing your own code.

Server debugging – a quick recap

Jenkins uses the `java.util.logging` package for logging; the details of this can be found here:

`https://docs.oracle.com/javase/7/docs/api/java/util/logging/package-summary.html`

The Jenkins documentation on logging is available here:

`https://wiki.jenkins-ci.org/display/JENKINS/Logging`

This page explains how to go about setting up your own custom log recorders — this can be very useful to separate and filter all the log output to help in finding what you are interested in, as *everything* is often piped to the default log, which can make analyzing difficult.

The Jenkins system log can be checked out using the user interface at **Manage Jenkins | System Log | All Jenkins Logs**, and there are also links to the RSS feeds available at the bottom of the page:

```
Oct 19, 2015 5:15:23 PM WARNING javax.jmdns.impl.DNSIncoming readAnswer
There was an OPT answer. Not currently handled. Option code: 65002 data: 24365E06B2A885CC

                                               All  > SEVERE  > WARNING




                              Page generated: 19-Oct-2015 17:23:50   REST API   Jenkins ver. 1.628
```

These can help identify and filter the different types of events within the system.

For issues with slave nodes, there are log files available in the following location: `~/.jenkins/logs/slaves/{slavename}`.

For job issues, historic log files are kept at `~/.jenkins/jobs/{jobname}/builds/{jobnumber}`.

You can also start Jenkins at a specific logging level by adding an additional -D argument to your startup process:

```
-Djava.util.logging.loglevel={level}
```

Here, `level` is one of the following:

- `SEVERE (highest value)`
- `WARNING`
- `INFO`
- `CONFIG`
- `FINE`
- `FINER`
- `FINEST (lowest value)`

The `Off` and `All` levels are also available—see this page for further details and options:

`http://docs.oracle.com/javase/7/docs/api/java/util/logging/Level.html`

Debugging with IntelliJ

To debug from within IntelliJ, point IntelliJ to the `pom.xml` file of the project and then select the option from the Run menu to create a new Run/Debug configuration. This should lead you to a screen similar to this:

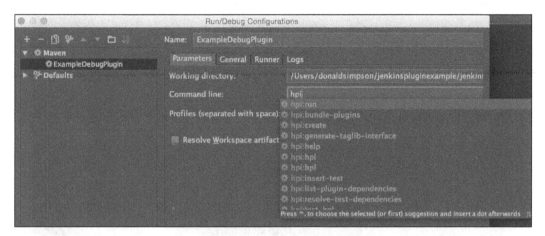

IntelliJ will have already parsed the POM file and will be aware of the available targets it contains. As soon as you start typing, for example, `hpi`, you would be presented with a drop-down list of all matching options to select from.

Select and run the required target (**hpi:run** again in this case) from the dropdown and then click on **Debug**.

You should see the familiar Jenkins startup process in the console and then be able to connect to a local debug session at:

`http://localhost:8080/jenkins`

Add a debug point to the code at the same place where we made our "Hello World" text change previously (double-click on the left margin of the line that says **hello world...** and then run the Jenkins job). This should run up to the break point you have set and produce this:

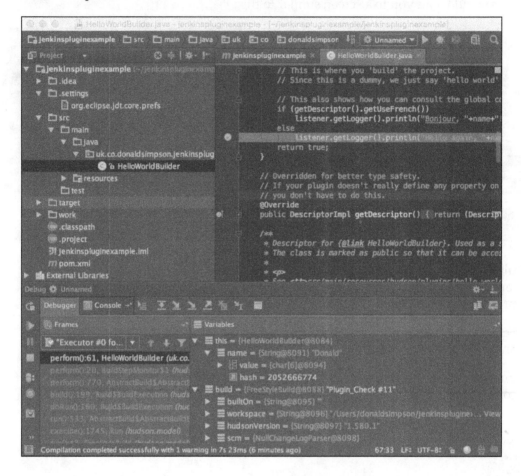

You can then use the debug arrows and buttons to drive through the debug process:

These allow you to step in to, over, or out of the current debug point, and you should be able to inspect the listed variables that are being updated to reflect the live state of the application being debugged.

For more information on debugging with IntelliJ, see this link:

`https://www.jetbrains.com/idea/help/stepping-through-the-program.html`

Debugging with Eclipse

Debugging with Eclipse is very similar to the process described for IntelliJ previously.

To set your breakpoint, double-click on the left-hand side margin in the code window, like this:

```
HelloWorldBuilder.java        jenkinspluginexample/pom.xml
56
57          // This also shows how you can consult the global configuration of
58          if (getDescriptor().getUseFrench())
59              listener.getLogger().println("Bonjour, "+name+"!");
60          else
61              listener.getLogger().println("Hello again, "+name+"!");
62          return true;
63      }
64
```

Next, right-click on the POM file in your Eclipse project and select **Debug as...** and the following window appears:

Specify the `hpi:run` target and then click on **Debug**; Jenkins should start up as usual in the Eclipse console window.

As before, point your browser to `http://localhost:8080/jenkins` and then create or run a job that hits the breakpoint you set earlier — when this code/point is reached, Jenkins will freeze and the focus will switch to Eclipse, where you can inspect the current state of the variables and properties and navigate through the various debugging steps to drill further into issues or step over areas to see what changes and happens.

mvnDebug

The `mvnDebug` tool provides an alternative approach that may be of interest to you. To use this, run `mvnDebug hpi:run` in the command line.

This should start up Maven in debug mode and a listener on port 8000 of local host, like this:

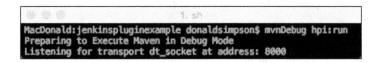

Now switch to your IDE and connect a debug session to this port. For example, in Eclipse, select **Run | Debug Configurations…**

This should produce the following window from which you can select **Remote Java Application**. Check whether the host and the port match:

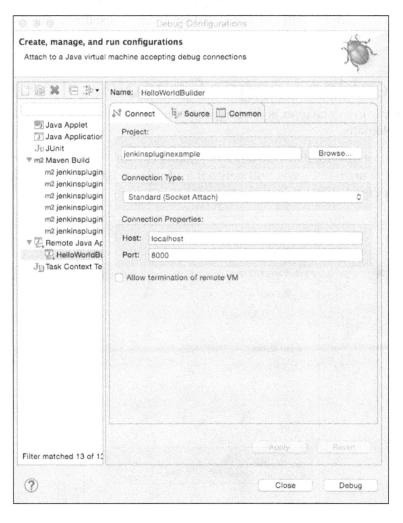

Next, select **Debug** to connect to the `mvnDebug` session you started in the console. At this point, the `hpi:run` target will start up (in the console) and run Jenkins in debug mode in Maven while connected to your chosen debugger—for example, Eclipse.

If you examine the `mvnDebug` executable, you will see that it simply sets `MAVEN_DEBUG_OPTS` before running the normal `mvn` binary, as follows:

```
MAVEN_DEBUG_OPTS="-Xdebug -Xrunjdwp:transport=dt_socket,server=y,suspe
nd=y,address=8000"
echo Preparing to Execute Maven in Debug Mode
env MAVEN_OPTS="$MAVEN_OPTS $MAVEN_DEBUG_OPTS" $(dirname $0)/mvn "$@"
```

This reveals that it would be easy to specify a different port if you wish, or you could adjust this script to add any additional parameters or settings you may want to include.

The Jenkins Logger Console

The final topic in this chapter is the **Logger Console** that is built in to the debug versions of Jenkins.

When you start up a local dev instance of Jenkins via Maven (whether through the command line or an IDE), you will notice the additional **Logger Console** box that is included on the left-hand side of the screen:

Expanding this box will reveal a **live** log output window, which you can customize in real time to adjust and filter in or out the types and severities of log items that you want to see or hide.

Keeping **info** selected provides a very verbose level of output, which includes information on mouseover events and other UI interactions. These can be very useful when debugging UI issues.

Unchecking the **info** box leaves just the **warn** and **error** messages. The log output can be managed by pausing and optionally clearing the output and adjusting the filters to suit your need. The following screenshot shows the **Logger Console**:

Summary

As you can see, there is a large range of options and approaches available for both testing and debugging within Jenkins. This chapter introduced some of the main tools and approaches that you may hopefully find useful for your own development processes.

Knowing how to test and debug your code and set up a productive development environment that suits your needs and preferences should improve the quality of your own development. It should also make things much easier further down the line, when you look at distributing your own plugin and are considering alternative development options. We will take a look at some alternative technologies and languages in the next chapter.

9
Putting Things Together

In this chapter, we will take a look at a selection of ways in which Jenkins can be extended by combining it with other languages, tools, and software.

In doing so, we will take a look at the following topics:

- Using the Jenkins script console
- Developing with Groovy, Grails, and Gradle
- Jenkins and Docker — Jenkins in Docker and Docker in Jenkins
- Building Android applications with Jenkins
- Building iOS applications with Jenkins

Covering all of these topics in detail is out of the scope of this book, but we will introduce the topics, explain the basic setup, and provide links for further information. This should provide a good enough overview and enable you to get started with using Jenkins with these technologies. Also, it may provide some ideas for extending your Jenkins setup to incorporate other tools and technologies.

The Jenkins script console and Groovy

The inbuilt script console is a very useful and powerful Jenkins extension and ideally suits certain types of tasks. This simple but powerful built-in web console allows you to run Groovy scripts on your Jenkins instance (or its slave nodes) from directly within the user interface, and is installed as standard.

To access the console, either navigate to **Manage Jenkins** and then select **Script Console**, or simply append `/script` to your Jenkins host and port, like this for example:

```
http://jenkinshost:8080/script
```

You should then be presented with a page similar to the following. This contains some introductory information and a link to the website `http://www.groovy-lang.org/` for further details on Groovy, the language that the script console uses.

This provided link is from the Jenkins home page:

```
https://wiki.jenkins-ci.org/display/JENKINS/Jenkins+Script+Console
```

It provides a useful collection of example scripts to show you how this works in order to get you started.

These example scripts cover a wide range of functions and are mostly focused on general Jenkins admin and housekeeping tasks—tasks that this tool suits very well due to its ease of use and flexibility. Using this interface, you can quickly and easily insert and edit code in a web page, run it with the click of a button, and see immediate results. There are no compilation steps or external dependencies to worry about.

For example, copying this Groovy code:

```
import hudson.model.*
import hudson.triggers.*
for(item in Hudson.instance.items) {
```

```
    for(trigger in item.triggers.values()) {
      if(trigger instanceof TimerTrigger) {
        println("--- Timer trigger for " + item.name + " ---")
        println(trigger.spec + '\n')
      }
    }
  }
}
```

After entering the example script at `https://wiki.jenkins-ci.org/display/ JENKINS/Display+timer+triggers` into the console and hitting **Run** will return the expected results — the details of all the scheduled jobs on this Jenkins instance (assuming you have some set up):

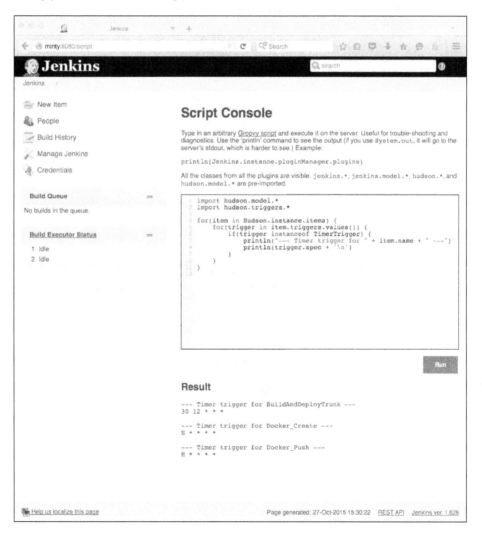

As you can see from this very simple example and the Groovy website, the Groovy language is aimed at Java developers and has a very flat learning curve. It is an extremely powerful tool and is well suited for certain tasks. It is often used in situations where developing and managing your own plugin is more than you really want or need. A simple Groovy script that can be run and altered on the fly can often be a better option for these tasks.

You can also create jobs that execute system Groovy scripts. These run within the Jenkins JVM, and therefore have access to the Jenkins internal objects and can interact with them.

This example details the setting up of a Groovy job that monitors the status of your slave nodes, refer to `http://www.donaldsimpson.co.uk/2013/06/07/ monitoring-jenkins-slave-nodes-with-groovy/` for more details.

The crux of this approach is the following simple Groovy code:

```
int exitcode = 0
for (slave in hudson.model.Hudson.instance.slaves) {
  if (slave.getComputer().isOffline().toString() == "true"){
    println('Slave ' + slave.name + " is offline!");
    exitcode++;
  }
}
if (exitcode > 0){
  println("We have a Slave down, failing the build!");
  return 1;
}
```

When added to a Jenkins job and run via a scheduled task, the Groovy code should exit with an error status whenever one or more of your existing slaves are offline, with the output being something along these lines:

```
Building on master in workspace /apps/jenkins/jobs/MonitorSlaves/
workspace Slave <YOURSLAVENAME> is offline!
We have a Slave down, failing the build!
Script returned: 1
Build step 'Execute system Groovy script' marked build as failure
Finished: FAILURE
```

This could obviously be extended to then perform whatever follow-up actions you want, for example, sending out an e-mail alert, or performing some other function (such as attempting to restart the slave or bringing a replacement slave online).

This link demonstrates an approach for automatically restarting offline slave nodes — it's written in Groovy too:

```
https://wiki.jenkins-ci.org/display/JENKINS/Monitor+and+Restart+Offli
ne+Slaves
```

Jenkins' built-in support for Groovy allows you to quickly and easily develop powerful custom scripts for your own needs. The Jenkins script console home page also details how you can run Groovy scripts remotely, and provides a list of available Jenkins plugins that use and support the Groovy language. These can be set up to allow you to run Groovy scripts as part of your builds.

Groovy and Gradle as alternatives

If you are interested in Groovy, you can also use this language and a combination of other tools to create your own plugins — you don't have to stick to Java and Maven if you don't want to.

This page explains how to modify your project to use a `build.gradle` file in place of the Maven POM file that we used previously:

```
http://jenkins-ci.org/content/gradle-fy-your-jenkins-plugin-project
```

You can then execute commands such as `gradle jpi`, `gradle check`, `gradle install`, and so on to build and manage the plugin life cycle without Maven.

This CloudBees presentation illustrates the use of Groovy instead of Java for the plugin itself:

```
https://www.cloudbees.com/event/topic/groovy-way-write-jenkins-plugin
```

This is an increasingly popular approach due to the power and simplicity of Groovy. It also explains how you can replace Jelly with Groovy — using the same language (Gradle is based on Groovy, so… it's all Groovy!) throughout the development process makes a lot of sense.

Jenkins and Docker

Docker is an application that enables you to package an application along with all of its dependencies into a single unit (a Docker **container**) that can be version controlled and deployed in an easy and standardized way.

The Docker home page explains how Docker works and how to install and use it:

```
https://www.docker.com/what-docker.
```

Conceptually, Docker containers are similar to lightweight virtual machines, but they have some fundamental architectural differences that make them more lightweight and more efficient, as illustrated by the following Docker and virtual machine comparison diagrams.

The following figure shows a normal virtual machine:

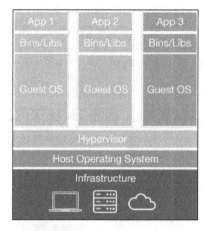

The following figure shows a Docker container:

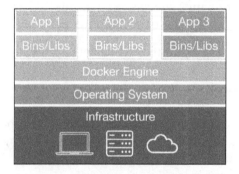

Docker containers can be published and managed with every change recorded. They are like highly efficient VMs managed under a version control system that provides functions similar to Git. They are also highly configurable and offer flexible and scalable deployment processes.

In addition to the auditing and ease of use, there is also a guarantee that containers will be (and behave) exactly the same on any environment that is capable of running Docker.

This can remove many of the environmental discrepancies that are normally associated with modern software development, eliminating the old *well, it works on my machine* syndrome, and the subtle variances between (supposedly identical) environments that sometimes cause serious and hard-to-detect issues.

Like Jenkins, Docker is extremely flexible, incredibly powerful, and highly extendable. Not surprisingly, they work extremely well together.

There are many ways in which you can combine and leverage the power of Docker and Jenkins. These approaches typically mean using either **Docker in Jenkins** or **Jenkins in Docker**.

Docker in Jenkins

Using the Docker plugin for Jenkins (`https://wiki.jenkins-ci.org/display/JENKINS/Docker+Plugin`), you can set up Jenkins jobs that can perform a guaranteed *clean build* every time in a fresh and known-good Docker container.

This can be done by dynamically provisioning a new slave node for the job to run on (pulled from a version-controlled **Docker Hub**).

The build or tests can then be run on this environment, and the results can be recorded and archived. The entire environment can then be deleted with the guarantee that, should you ever wish to, combining that very Docker container with the same version of the deployed code will recreate exactly the same results at any future date and on any environment.

Jenkins in Docker

We have previously looked at several different ways to set up and manage your Jenkins server. We have also stressed the importance of storing your Jenkins configuration in a version control system, and ensuring that you can recover from issues without losing data.

Extending Jenkins to take advantage of Docker enables you to rapidly and easily create (or recreate) your own Jenkins environment from a known-good snapshot. Simply by setting up and maintaining your Jenkins server within a Docker-managed container, you immediately gain all the advantages and abilities that Docker offers.

A popular, readymade Docker container for this approach is the CloudBees one here:

```
https://github.com/jenkinsci/docker
```

Once you have Docker installed and set up on your environment, all you need to do is run this command:

```
docker run -p 8080:8080 -p 50000:50000 jenkins
```

The `Dockerfile` on the following GitHub page details how this container is built and some of the many alternative approaches and options that you can use and adapt:

```
https://github.com/jenkinsci/docker/blob/master/Dockerfile
```

Once you have Jenkins running in Docker, you can make any changes that you may want, and then publish a snapshot of your altered version under your own account on the Docker Hub, effectively version controlling the entire setup. If you prefer, you can even create and maintain your own local version of the Docker Hub (running on Docker, of course) and publish/pull your own images to and from there.

Docker containers do not persist their data once the container itself dies—you need to save the state and publish it. As mentioned on the GitHub page though, you can set up persistent storage by mounting data volumes from the local filesystem (that is, a specified folder on the host running Docker). The contents of these folders (which could contain configuration information, public keys, or plugin data for example) can be pulled from and managed by version control too. Alternatively, you can create your own dedicated volume container that would allow you to manage all of the persistent data within another Docker container. This can also be version controlled and attached to your Jenkins containers as and when required.

You can also set up your Jenkins slaves to run on dynamically provisioned Docker slaves. There are a number of Jenkins plugins for doing this, and as this is a rapidly evolving technology, there are bound to be many more, for example, this plugin:

```
https://wiki.jenkins-ci.org/display/JENKINS/Docker+Slaves+Plugin
```

This detailed post on creating Jenkins slave Docker images for dynamic provisioning is available at:

```
https://developer.jboss.org/people/pgier/blog/2014/06/30/on-demand-
jenkins-slaves-using-docker
```

These are just a few of the (currently) most common ways of combining Jenkins and Docker; there are many other possibilities and more are bound to evolve soon. You could, for example, run your main Jenkins instance inside a Docker container and have it run Jenkins jobs that create other Docker containers to run your tests and builds, which in turn could use Docker containers!

There is even a **Docker in Docker** project, which allows you to create and manage Docker containers from inside Docker containers… many interesting possibilities!

Jenkins and Android

Jenkins can, with the help of an SDK and a few plugins, be set up to automate the building, deployment, testing, and publishing of Android applications. To build Android applications, you need the Android software development kit, which you can download from:

```
http://developer.android.com/sdk/index.html
```

When it is downloaded, extract the archive to a local directory. Then edit and add the following environment variables to your system:

```
export ANDROID_HOME="<location of extracted files>"
export PATH="$ANDROID_HOME/tools:$ANDROID_HOME/platform-tools:$PATH"
```

Once this is done, update the SDK and verify that your Jenkins user has read and execute permissions on the SDK executable files.

To run an Android emulator as part of your build process, add this plugin to your Jenkins server:

```
https://wiki.jenkins-ci.org/display/JENKINS/Android+Emulator+Plugin
```

Note that this will attempt to install an Android SDK for you if it doesn't find one. It's often preferable to set up the SDK, as per your requirement, in advance though. You can disable the autoinstall attempt through the **Automatically install Android components when required** option on the **Manage Jenkins** settings page, and specify which SDK it should use here:

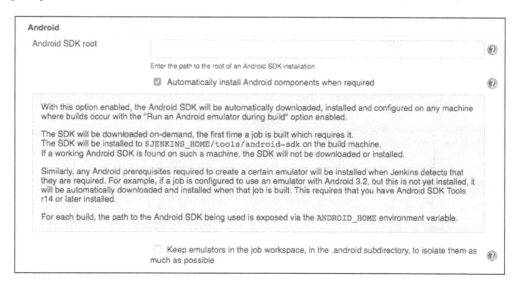

As described in the Android emulator plugin instructions, you should then be able to create a new Jenkins job that runs an Android emulator during the build with whatever hardware and software specification you would like to use. You can specify the memory, screen size and resolution, OS version, and so on, as shown here:

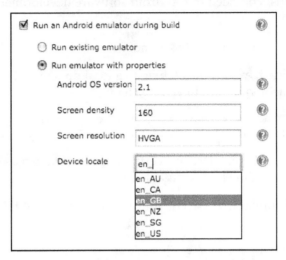

(Source: https://wiki.jenkins-ci.org/download/attachments/43712988/android_job-custom.png?version=1&modificationDate=1270447137000)

Your Jenkins job can then proceed to install your recently compiled application using the Android `adb` command-line tool, like this for example:

```
adb install my-app.apk
```

Alternatively, you can specify a new build step that will (re)install the APK for you, as shown in the following diagram:

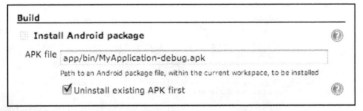

(Image taken from https://wiki.jenkins-ci.org/download/attachments/43712988/android_install-package.png?version=1&modificationDate=1299432099000)

After the application is deployed, you can include an additional test step to run the Android Monkey Tester tool. This will run your tests against the latest APK running on the Android emulator, which will emulate whatever hardware and software specifications you have selected. It's often useful to set up multiple jobs to ensure that your tests cover all the combinations and permutations of hardware and software that your users may have.

There is also a Jenkins plugin that enables you to automatically publish and roll out your built application to the Google Play store:

```
https://wiki.jenkins-ci.org/display/JENKINS/Google+Play+Android+Publisher+Plugin
```

For further details on building, deploying, and testing Android applications with Jenkins, this link is a great place to start:
```
https://wiki.jenkins-ci.org/display/JENKINS/Building+an+Android+app+and+test+project
```

Jenkins and iOS

Your Jenkins setup and scope can also be extended to build iOS projects in a very similar way to the preceding steps for Android. The general idea is the same; install and configure an SDK (XCode for iOS), add the required Jenkins plugin, build and deploy the application on an emulator, run the tests against it, and record the outcome.

However, one important distinction for iOS builds is that you need an OS X host to run it on. This host can be set up as a Jenkins slave node though, with your iOS-based Jenkins jobs set to run on that node only.

The host will need a local installation of XCode, which is available here:

```
https://developer.apple.com/xcode/download/
```

Or it is available from within the Apple App Store.

This Jenkins page covers the installation and setup process in detail:

```
https://wiki.jenkins-ci.org/display/JENKINS/Xcode+Plugin
```

And here are a few additional links for further information on iOS and Jenkins:

- `http://savvyapps.com/blog/continuous-integration-ios-jenkins`
- `https://www.built.io/blog/2014/10/how-to-set-up-customized-jenkins-for-ios/`
- `http://blog.pivotal.io/labs/labs/ios-ci-jenkins`
- `http://youandthegang.com/2015/continuous-integration-delivery-with-jenkins/`

Keeping your Jenkins version and plugins up to date

As with all modern software, it is important to keep your Jenkins version and plugins up to date.

You can subscribe to plugin release notifications via RSS here: `http://feeds.feedburner.com/JenkinsPluginReleases`

Otherwise, you can subscribe here: `https://jenkins-ci.org/releases.rss`

You can follow Jenkins release notifications on Twitter at this link: `https://twitter.com/jenkins_release`

Summary

From the brief introductions and examples in this chapter, we have seen how easily Jenkins can be extended and adapted to work and integrate with other languages and technologies, taking advantage of what they offer and allowing you to set up processes that work the way you want and need them to. Combining Jenkins with other tools enables you to create powerful and flexible build processes for a wide variety of projects and purposes.

Jenkins integrates well with these technologies (and many others), largely due to its inherent flexibility and extensibility, its wealth of plugins, and the vibrant development, support, and user community.

Throughout this book, we have explored many different ways in which Jenkins can be adapted and extended to perform whatever functions you would like, from leveraging APIs, interacting through IDEs, and adapting the user interface to developing your own plugin, creating and using extension points, to embracing and leveraging new and emerging technologies.

Hopefully, these topics and skills will encourage and empower you to find new and interesting ways to leverage the power of Jenkins for your own projects.

Index

extension annotation
  reference link 66
Extension Indexer program
  about 91
  reference link 91
Extension Points 60

G

Git 9
Google Play Android Publisher Plugin
  reference link 127
Gradle
  using 121
Green Balls plugin
  reference link 104
Groovy
  about 118, 120
  references 120
  using 121

H

help*.html files 98
Hub 123

I

i18n internationalization
  reference link 98
implements keyword 61
information
  obtaining, from Jenkins 46, 47
  radiating 50
Information Radiator
  creating, with Jenkins XML API 46
installation, Maven 71-75
installation, Mylyn 34
IntelliJ
  debugging with 109-111
IntelliJ IDEA 38
interface keyword 61
interfaces
  about 61
  using 63
internationalization
  reference link 98

iOS
  references 128
iOS applications
  developing, with Jenkins 127

J

Java Development Kit (JDK) 9
Java IDE 9
java.util.logging package
  reference link 107
JAXP 48
Jelly
  about 97
  reference link 98
Jenkins
  about 2, 97
  and Docker 121-123
  Android applications, developing
    with 125-127
  configuring 35-38
  debugging 107
  debugging, basics 86, 87
  Docker, using for 123
  evolution 7, 8
  extension, declaring in 66
  information, obtaining from 46, 47
  iOS applications, developing with 127
  keeping up to date 128
  references 118, 128
  running, basics 86, 87
  tools, for extending 9
  use case scenarios 13-28
  using, as web server 50, 51
  using, for Docker 123, 124
Jenkins build connectors 38-41
Jenkins CLI
  about 52
  remote jobs, triggering via 53-55
  setting up 52
  using 53
Jenkins configuration
  updating 56
Jenkins Control Plugin 38
Jenkins in Docker 123
JenkinsLinuxStartupScript
  reference link 5

standard Jenkins instance
  deploying to 78-85
Stapler
  about 96
  reference link 97
starting point
  building 95
  loading 95
Subversion repository
  references 26
Swarm plugin
  reference link 23

T

testing scenarios, Jenkins
  reference link 107
tests
  running, with Maven 104-107
tools, for extending Jenkins
  Git 9
  Java Development Kit (JDK) 9
  Java IDE 9
  Jenkins Source 9
  Maven 9
  Mylyn 9

U

use case scenarios, Jenkins
  large number of jobs 13-19
  multiple hosts 20-23
  UI tweaks 27, 28
  users, helping through UI
    automation 24-27
userContent directory 50

V

versions, IDEs
  references 9
Views functionality 27

W

web server
  Jenkins, using as 50, 51

X

XCode
  references, for installing 127
XmlParser 48
XML::Simple 48

Thank you for buying
Extending Jenkins

About Packt Publishing

Packt, pronounced 'packed', published its first book, *Mastering phpMyAdmin for Effective MySQL Management*, in April 2004, and subsequently continued to specialize in publishing highly focused books on specific technologies and solutions.

Our books and publications share the experiences of your fellow IT professionals in adapting and customizing today's systems, applications, and frameworks. Our solution-based books give you the knowledge and power to customize the software and technologies you're using to get the job done. Packt books are more specific and less general than the IT books you have seen in the past. Our unique business model allows us to bring you more focused information, giving you more of what you need to know, and less of what you don't.

Packt is a modern yet unique publishing company that focuses on producing quality, cutting-edge books for communities of developers, administrators, and newbies alike. For more information, please visit our website at www.packtpub.com.

About Packt Open Source

In 2010, Packt launched two new brands, Packt Open Source and Packt Enterprise, in order to continue its focus on specialization. This book is part of the Packt Open Source brand, home to books published on software built around open source licenses, and offering information to anybody from advanced developers to budding web designers. The Open Source brand also runs Packt's Open Source Royalty Scheme, by which Packt gives a royalty to each open source project about whose software a book is sold.

Writing for Packt

We welcome all inquiries from people who are interested in authoring. Book proposals should be sent to author@packtpub.com. If your book idea is still at an early stage and you would like to discuss it first before writing a formal book proposal, then please contact us; one of our commissioning editors will get in touch with you.

We're not just looking for published authors; if you have strong technical skills but no writing experience, our experienced editors can help you develop a writing career, or simply get some additional reward for your expertise.

Jenkins Essentials

ISBN: 978-1-78355-347-1   Paperback: 186 pages

Continuous Integration – setting up the stage for a DevOps culture

1. Explore continuous integration and automation, along with how to manage and configure Jenkins.

2. Discover the process of using Jenkins to build, test, and package Java applications.

3. Learn about the extensible features of Jenkins with the use of advanced plugins.

Jenkins Continuous Integration Cookbook
Second Edition

ISBN: 978-1-78439-008-2   Paperback: 408 pages

Over 90 recipes to produce great results from Jenkins using pro-level practices, techniques, and solutions

1. Explore the use of more than 40 best-of-breed plugins for improving efficiency.

2. Secure and maintain Jenkins by integrating it with LDAP and CAS, which is a Single Sign-on solution.

3. Step-by-step, easy-to-use instructions to optimize the existing features of Jenkins using the complete set of plugins that Jenkins offers.

Jenkins Continuous Integration Cookbook

ISBN: 978-1-84951-740-9   Paperback: 344 pages

Over 80 recipes to maintain, secure, communicate, test, build, and improve the software development process with Jenkins

1. Explore the use of more than 40 best of breed plugins.

2. Use code quality metrics, integration testing through functional and performance testing to measure the quality of your software.

3. Get a problem-solution approach enriched with code examples for practical and easy comprehension.

Cucumber Cookbook

ISBN: 978-1-78528-600-1   Paperback: 162 pages

Over 35 hands-on recipes to efficiently master the art of behaviour-driven development using Cucumber-JVM

1. Create a test automation framework to handle web, REST, and native mobile application automation.

2. Discover Glue code, Hooks, Tags, and Cucumber's integration with Maven, Jenkins, and Git.

3. Comprehensive recipes in Cucumber for behaviour-driven development and test automation.

Please check **www.PacktPub.com** for information on our titles